FILIPINO TEACHERS PRACTICES ON MULTI-MODAL LITERACY AND GLOBAL CITIZENSHIP EDUCATION:

BASIS FOR A PROPOSED CAPACITY BUILDING PROGRAM

BY

PROF. CARMELITA DG. SERRANO LPT, PhD

BY: PROF. CARMELITA DG. SERRANO

ISBN:

Hardbound-978-621-495-176-5

Softbound/Paperback-978-621-495-177-2

MOBI/KINDLE-978-621-495-178-9

Published by:

Poetry Planet Book Publishing House

Rosario, Pozorrubio, Pangasinan, Philippines

Contact Number:075-615-545

Email: maritesritumalta@gmail.com

DEDICATION

This published research study is especially dedicated to my loved ones who truly inspire me to work hard and passionately extend their help and effort in the success of my work. To my dearest husband Mr. Michael S. Serrano, my inspiration and my support throughout my career path in finishing this study, I am deeply extending my gratefulness in sharing these sacrifices of my work.

To my children Carl Michael Serrano, Carrie Mikaella Serrano and Carrisse Michaela Serrano, to my dearest auntie Edna Dela Cruz, to my niece Cryzhiane Nicole Caliso, to our furbabies Sky, Storm, Thunder, Shimmer, Shine, and Winter who became my inspiration why I strive hard to finish my studies.

To my beloved mother Florentina Tuaño De Guzman Rana, I succeeded because of all the values you taught me since childhood that have become my shield in all the ventures in life.

Finally, I would like to dedicate this to Almighty God for the grace given to me as I embark on this journey with all the hardships that make me strong and the success to complete this masterpiece of wisdom bestowed upon me.

-CDGS

ABSTRACT

FILIPINO TEACHERS PRACTICES ON MULTI-MODAL LITERACY AND GLOBAL CITIZENSHIP EDUCATION: BASIS FOR A PROPOSED CAPACITY BUILDING PROGRAM

The integration of multi-modal literacy and global citizenship education (GCE) is crucial in preparing students for the complexities of the modern world. This study investigated the practices of Filipino teachers concerning multimodal literacy and global citizenship education. It aims to lay the groundwork for a proposed capacity-building program. By understanding current practices, the proposed program can tailor its approach to enhance teacher capacity in these critical areas, ultimately enriching educational experiences for Filipino students.

This study also investigated the multimodal literacy of Filipino teachers in KS3 (Key Stage 3) and its relationship to learner citizenship. It explores the demographic profile of teacher respondents (age, gender, experience, etc.) and assesses their multimodal literacy (including multicultural and multilingual aspects) from three perspectives: master teachers, school heads, and the teachers themselves. The research examined if these groups have significantly different assessments. Additionally, the study explores the perceived level of citizenship (national and global) among learners according to the three respondent groups and investigates the potential link between teacher multimodal literacy and learner citizenship. Furthermore, the study identifies challenges faced by teachers in implementing multimodal literacy practices and proposes a capacity-building program based on the findings.

The study utilized the multi-method approach and quantitative data collection research using a survey questionnaire as its data gathering instrument. The respondents of the study were four hundred fifty teachers from the three divisions of Caloocan City, Valenzuela and Manila chosen through Slovin's formula to get the number of respondents. The statistical tools employed were frequency, percentage, weighted mean, ranking, and ANOVA.

According to the gathered data, the teaching staff leaned female, with an average age of 41-45. Most teachers held Master's degrees, had 11-15 years of experience, and actively participated in professional development seminars. Master teachers, school heads, and teachers themselves all rated Filipino teachers' multi-cultural (3.73) and multilingual literacy (3.77) very high. Interestingly, while all three groups agreed on the high level of multimodal literacy, their assessments significantly differed based on teacher profiles in terms of gender, length of service, position, educational attainment, and area of specialization. Age, however, did not show a significant influence on the assessment. Learners were perceived to possess very high levels of both global and national citizenship according to all respondent groups. There was a significant positive relationship between teacher multimodal literacy level and the profile groupings, and between teacher literacy and learner citizenship. A major finding was the very high level of challenges encountered by teachers in implementing multimodal literacy practices.

The findings indicate that while Filipino teachers are incorporating various forms of literacy—including digital, visual, and textual—into their teaching, there is significant variability in implementation. Many teachers demonstrate innovative practices but face challenges such as limited resources, inadequate training, and varying levels of student engagement. In terms of GCE, teachers often incorporate global themes but struggle to fully integrate these concepts into the curriculum due to a lack of structured guidelines and support.

The research highlighted the significant role of multimodal literacy in education and its positive correlation with learner citizenship. By highlighting the challenges and proposing a structured capacity-building program, to support teachers in enhancing their multi-modal literacy and GCE practices, it provides actionable insights for improving educational practices and policies in the context of Filipino KS3 teachers. The use of statistical tools and a comprehensive demographic analysis adds depth to the findings, making the study a valuable contribution to the field of education. The actionable insights derived from this research can guide policymakers, educational leaders, and practitioners in creating supportive environments that promote effective multimodal literacy practices, ultimately leading to improved educational outcomes and more engaged global citizens.

TABLE OF CONTENTS

TITLE **PAGE**

Chapter I

THE PROBLEM AND IT'S BACKGROUND 9

Introduction 9

Background of the Study 11

Statement of the Problem 15

Hypotheses 16

Scope and Delimitation of the Study 17

Significance of the Study 18

Chapter 2

REVIEW OF RELATED LITERATURE AND STUDIES 20

Synthesis of the Reviewed Studies 43

Theoretical Framework 45

Theoretical Paradigm of the Study .... **Error! Bookmark not defined.**

Conceptual Framework 48

Conceptual Paradigm of the Study .... **Error! Bookmark not defined.**

Definition of Terms 50

Chapter 3

RESEARCH DESIGN AND METHODOLOGY 52

Research Design 52

Population and Sampling Technique 53

Research Instrument 53

Data Gathering Procedure 54

Statistical Treatment of Data 54

Chapter 4

PRESENTATION, ANALYSIS, AND INTERPRETATION OF DATA 56

1. Profile of the Teacher Respondents by Frequency and Percentage 56

2. Multi-modal literacy practices of Filipino teachers........................63
3. Significant difference in the assessment of the respondents on the extent of multimodal literacy practices of Filipino teachers..................69
4. Significant relationship between the extent of multimodal literacy practices of Filipino teachers when grouped according to profile........71
5. Assessment of the respondents on the teachers practices of citizenship education in terms of the following: 72
6. Significant difference in the assessment of the respondents in the extent of teachers citizenship education. 78
7. Significant relationship between the extent of multi-modal literacy of Filipino teachers and the level of citizenship education.......................79
8. Challenges encountered by respondents on the practice of............80
Multi-modal literacy..80
9. Proposed Capacity Building Plan..83
Chapter 5
SUMMARY OF FINDINGS, CONCLUSIONS, AND RECOMMENDATIONS..84
Summary Of Findings..84
Conclusions...90
Recommendations...91
Bibliography...94
APPENDICES A..96
THE AUTHOR..99

Chapter I

THE PROBLEM AND IT'S BACKGROUND

This chapter presents the introduction, background of the study, statement of the problem, hypotheses, scope and delimitation, and significance of the study.

Introduction

In the ever-evolving landscape of education, the intersection of technology, language, and culture becomes increasingly vital for fostering global citizens equipped with the necessary skills to navigate the complexities of the 21st century. This study delves into the realm of Multimodal Literacy within the context of the revised K to 10 curriculum, otherwise known as the Matatag curriculum, with a keen focus on its implications for the development of national and global citizenship. Under the Matatag curriculum, lessons from kindergartento Grade 10 will focus on five foundational skills, which are language, reading and literacy, mathematics, makabansa, and good manners and right conduct, which is in contrast with the seven learning areas offered in the previous curriculum, that are mother tongue, Filipino, English, Mathematics, Araling Panlipunan, Mapeh, and Edukasyon sa Pagpapakatao.

As the Philippines positions itself in an interconnected world, therole of educators in nurturing students' multimodal literacy skills takes on heightened significance.

In today's interconnected world, being literate goes beyond traditional reading and writing skills. Multi-modal literacy, which encompasses the ability to understand and create meaning through various modes of communication, is becoming increasingly important. According to the study conducted by Ong (2019), multi-modal literacy is essential in preparing students for the challenges and opportunities of the 21st century. It enables them to effectively navigate and communicate in a digital and globalized society. Multimodal literacy involves the ability to comprehend, analyze, and produce communication in various modes, such as visual, auditory, gestural, and spatial. It goes beyond traditional literacy paradigms, encompassing a broader spectrum of communication channels that are integral to contemporary society. Understanding how Filipino Key Stage three students engage with multimodal literacy is crucial for designing effective educational strategies that align with the demands of the globalized information age.

The Department of Education (DepEd) recognizes the significance of multimodal literacy in the Filipino education system. In accordance with the new Matatag Curriculum, language, reading, and literacy are emphasized as key components of the curriculum in Key Stage Three Filipino education. This order highlights the need to develop student's skills in interpreting and creating meaning across different modes of communication, such as visual, auditory, and digital media.

Under the Matatag curriculum, teachers are tasked with guiding students in developing five foundational skills: language, reading and literacy, mathematics, makabansa, and good manners and right conduct. This streamlined approach focuses on essential areas of learning compared to the previous curriculum, which had seven learning areas. To effectively implement the Matatag curriculum, teachers need to deeply understand multimodal literacy and its implications for national and global citizenship. They play a vital role in equipping students with the necessary tools to navigate the complexities of the 21st century. To support teachers in this endeavor, a comprehensive capacity-building program is proposed. This program aims to enhance teachers' understanding and application of multimodal literacy within the Filipino curriculum. By equipping teachers with the necessary tools and strategies, they can effectively guide and empower students to become effective communicators in an interconnected world.

To develop the proposed capacity-building program, a thorough review of existing literature on multimodal literacy and its relevance to Filipino education will be conducted. According to Santos (2018), incorporating multimodal literacy in the classroom enhances students' critical thinking skills, creativity, and engagement with the subject matter. Additionally, Gomez (2020) highlights the importance of multimodal literacy in preparing students for the challenges and opportunities of the 21st century.

Moreover, surveys will be conducted with teachers to gather insights on their experiences and perspectives regarding multimodal literacy in the Filipino curriculum. This qualitative and quantitative data will provide valuable information on the challenges faced by teachers and the aspirations of students in developing their multimodal literacy skills.

The findings of this study will contribute to the development of a capacity building program that aligns with the needs and goals of the Matatag curriculum. By focusing on the teachers' role in implementing multimodal literacy, this program aims to empower teachers to effectively guide students in becoming competent and responsible citizens who can contribute to nation-building and global development.

Background of the Study

The Filipino practices in multi-modal literacy and global citizenship education is rooted in the evolving educational landscape of the Philippines, which is increasingly recognizing the importance of integrating global competencies into its curriculum. Global citizenship education (GCED) in the Philippines has been gaining traction as part of the country's efforts to align with international educational standards and frameworks, such as those promoted by UNESCO and he United Nations' Global Education First Initiative. The Philippines' Department of Education (DepEd) has been actively working to integrate topics related to global citizenship and inclusivity into the K-12 curriculum. This initiative aims to equip students with the knowledge, skills, and values necessary to engage in an interconnected and interdependent world.

Current studies indicate that while the Philippines is still in the process of formally adopting a comprehensive GCED framework, there are already elements of global citizenship embedded within existing subjects like social studies and values education. For instance, the Southeast Asia Primary Learning Metrics (SEA-PLM) assessment has been used to evaluate Filipino students' global competencies, revealing insights into their knowledge, attitudes, beliefs, and behavioral intentions regarding global issues.

In terms of multi-modal literacy, the educational approach in the Philippines increasingly incorporates diverse forms of media and communication methods to enhance learning. This includes the use of digital platforms, multimedia resources, and interactive teaching strategies to develop students' critical thinking and problem-solving skills in various contexts.

The proposed capacity-building program aims to further develop these competencies by providing educators with the necessary training and resources to effectively teach and integrate multi-modal literacy and GCED into their classrooms. This program would likely focus on professional development, curriculum enhancement, and the creation of supportive educational policies to foster a more inclusive and globally-minded educational environment in the Philippines.

The Department of Education (DepEd) officially launched the revised curriculum for Kindergarten to Grade 10 (K to 10), under the K to 12 Program, on August 10, 2023. This curriculum is known as the MATATAG curriculum. In an interview with Manila Bulletin, Vice President Sarah Duterte explained the meaning behind the acronym. According to Duterte, the "MA" in MATATAG stands for "Makabagong kurikulum na napapanahon" which translates to "modern and relevant curriculum."

The goal is to provide learners with knowledge and skills that are up-todate and responsive to the demands of globalization. Duterte emphasized the importance of offering relevant knowledge and developing skills that are applicable in a constantly evolving world.

The first "TA" in MATATAG represents "Talino na mula sa isip at puso" which means "intelligence from the mind and heart." Duterte explained that this promotes a balance between intellectual intelligence and emotional maturity.

Learners need to be mentally prepared to face challenges and emotionally ready to navigate the complexities of life. The second "TA" in MATATAG stands for "Tapang na humarap sa ano man ang hamon sa buhay" which translates to "courage to face life's challenges." This aspect of the curriculum aims to harness the deep sense of identity as Filipinos and prepare learners to confront uncertainties and adversities as a nation. Duterte expressed the hope of seeing learners grow into patriotic citizens. Lastly, the "G" in MATATAG represents "Galing ng Pilipino, nangingibabaw sa mundo" which means "excellence of Filipinos, shining in the world." The objective is to produce learners who are ready and equipped with the necessary knowledge and skills to excel on the global stage (Hernando-Malipot, 2022). The MATATAG Agenda was launched as the new direction of the Department of Education (DepEd) towards improving the quality of basic education in the country.

To help attain the commitments articulated in the MATATAG Agenda, DepEd has adopted DepEd Order (DO) No. 013, s. 2023, Adoption of the National Learning Recovery Program (NLRP) in the Department of Education. This includes the implementation of the revised curriculum, otherwise known as the MATATAG Curriculum. The MATATAG Curriculum has the features decongested curriculum, focus on foundational skills, balanced cognitive demands, clearer articulation of 2lst-century skills, reduced learning areas, intensified Values Education and Peace Education, and on par with international standards (DepEd, 2023). The DepEd will introduce the new curriculum in phases, first to kindergarten, grades 1, 4, and 7 in the 2024-2025 school year. This will be followed by grades 2, 5, and 8 in 2025; then 3, 6, and 9 in 2026, and grade 10 by 2027. By 2028, the DepEd expects full implementation of the new curriculum (Macasero, 2023).

However, before its phased implementation, the MATATAG Curriculum is piloted in selected schools in Regions I, II, VII, and XII, the Cordillera

Administrative Region (CAR), the CARAGA region, and the National Capital Region (NCR) starting SY 2023-2024, based on the DepEd Memorandum No. 54, s. 2023 called "Pilot implementation of the Matatag Curriculum" The main feature of the revised K to 10 curriculum is reducing the number of competencies making it a leaner version of the current curriculum. DepEd will give greater emphasis on the development of foundational skills, such as literacy, numeracy, and socioemotional skills (Hernando-Malipot, 2022).

In the context of the revised curriculum, the emphasis on foundational skills suggests a recognition of the essential building blocks required for a well-rounded education.

This parallels the notion of Multi-modal Literacy, which likely involves a broader and more inclusive approach to literacy that goes beyond traditional reading and writing. The focus on socio-emotional skills also indicates a recognition of the importance of holistic development, which is crucial for fostering global citizenship. In the proposed capacity-building program for teachers, there might be an opportunity to integrate the principles of the revised curriculum. This could involve training educators to effectively implement multi-modal literacy strategies that align with the curriculum's emphasis on foundational skills. Teachers could also receive guidance on incorporating socio-emotional learning into their teaching practices to better prepare students for national and global citizenship. By linking the revised K to 10 curriculum's goals with the proposed capacity-building program for teachers in Multi-modal Literacy, there is potential for a more coherent and integrated educational approach that addresses the evolving needs of students in the context of a changing global landscape.

Statement of the Problem

This study aimed to determine Filipino Teachers Practices on Multi-Modal Literacy and Global Citizenship Education: Basis for a Proposed Capacity Building Program among selected divisions in the National Capital Region particularly the Division of Caloocan, Manila, and Valenzuela.

This study also sought to answer the following questions:

1. What is the demographic profile of the Filipino teachers respondents in terms of:

    1.1 age;

    1.2 gender;

    1.3 length of service;

    1.4 plantilla position;

    1.5 highest educational attainment;

    1.6 area of specialization and

    1.7 relevant seminars and training attended?

2. What is the extent of multi-modal literacy practices of Filipino teachers as assessed by master teachers, school heads/head teachers, and teachers themselves in teachers in terms of::

    2.1 Multi-cultural Literacy and

    2.2 Multilingual literacy?

3. Is there a significant difference in the assessment of the respondents on the extent of multimodal literacy practices of Filipino teachers based on the aforementioned variables?

4. Is there a significant relationship between the extents of multimodal literacy practices of Filipino teachers when grouped according to profile?

5. What is the assessment of the respondents on the teachers' practices of citizenship education in terms of the following:

5.1 National and

5.2 Global?

6. Is there a significant difference in the assessment of respondents in the extent of citizenship education based on the aforementioned variables?

7. Is there a significant relationship between the extent of multi-modal literacy practices of teachers and the teachers' practices of citizenship education?

8. What are the challenges encountered by the respondents to the following practices of multi-modal literacy?

9. Based on the findings of the study, what capacity-building program for teachers may be proposed?

Hypotheses

The following hypotheses are to be tested at 0.05 level of significance.

H01: There is no significant significant difference in the assessment of the respondents on the extent of multimodal literacy practices of Filipino teachers based on the aforementioned variables.

H02: There is no significant relationship between the extent of multimodal literacy practices of Filipino teachers when grouped according to profile

H03: There is no significant difference in the assessment of respondents in the extent of citizenship education based on the aforementioned variables.

H04: There is no significant relationship between the extent of multimodal literacy practices of teachers and the teachers' practices of citizenship education.

Scope and Delimitation of the Study

The study is conducted from school year 2023 to 2024. The researcher aims to provide a clear and manageable framework for examining the practices of Filipino teachers and developing a targeted capacity building program for Teachers in, NCR, in terms of, the assessment of the three groups of respondents in the level of multimodal literacy of Filipino teachers. Moreover, the respondents were limited to teachers, and Master Teachers of the selected schools in Manila, Valenzuela, and Caloocan City.

The study will be limited to Multimodal Literacy within the context of the revised K to 10 curriculum, otherwise known as the Matatag curriculum, with a keen focus on its implications for the development of national and global citizenship in Public Secondary Schools. The research study will be applied to the target population. The study population consisted of all teachers, master teachers and head teachers in the three chosen division namely Caloocan, Valenzuela and Manila. A convenient sample of four hundred fifty (450) subjects was selected from the three division.

The sample included three hundred seventy-five (375) teachers, forty-five (45) master teachers and thirty (30) head teachers. Available subjects were entered into the study until a sample size of 450 was reached. Subjects who met the sample criteria were identified by the researcher at the three divisions.

The scope of this study encompassed the investigation of the current practices of Filipino teachers in integrating multi-modal literacy and global citizenship education (GCE) within their teaching methodologies. It focused on teachers from various regions in the Philippines, ensuring a diverse representation from urban, suburban, and rural areas, and includes educators from elementary to high school levels across both public and private institutions. The study aims to explore how teachers utilize various modes of literacy—textual, digital, visual, and auditory—to enhance student learning, and to what extent these modalities are integrated into the curriculum and instructional practices.

Additionally, it assessed how teachers incorporated GCE to foster students' understanding of global issues, intercultural competence, social justice, and sustainable development. Based on these findings, the study proposed a capacity-building program designed to enhance teachers' skills and knowledge in multi-modal literacy and GCE, including professional development workshops, resource materials, and ongoing support mechanisms.

The delimitations of this study defined its boundaries to maintain focused and managed the research scope effectively. Participant selection limited to a specific sample size of teachers who voluntarily agreed to participate, which may not fully represented the entire population of Filipino teachers. Data was collected primarily through surveys, interviews, and classroom observations, without employing experimental methods or longitudinal studies due to time and resource constraints. The research was conducted within a defined period, typically spanning one academic year, limiting the ability to observe the long-term impacts of current practices or the proposed capacity-building program. The study specifically focused on multi-modal literacy and GCE, and other aspects of teaching practices, such as subject-specific pedagogies or administrative duties, not been the primary focused unless directly related to the main areas of interest. Furthermore, the research considered the varying levels of access to technology and resources among different schools and regions, which influenced the feasibility and effectiveness of multi-modal literacy practices.

Significance of the Study

The results of the research are expected to be beneficial for the following group of people.

Learners. As primary stakeholders in the educational system, directly benefit from this research in multifaceted ways. The study on multi-modal literacy aims to provide learners with a more engaging and diverse learning experience, incorporating various modes of communication and expression. This can lead to increased interest, participation, and a deeper understanding of the subject matter. By developing multi-modal literacy skills, learners are better equipped to communicate effectively in a global context. This prepares them for active participation as responsible citizens in a world that increasingly demands cross-cultural understanding and collaboration.

Academic institutions and administrators. Since they play a pivotal role in shaping the educational landscape, the study contributes to the enhancement of the curriculum by promoting multi-modal literacy. Academic institutions can integrate these findings into their educational frameworks, ensuring that students receive a well-rounded education that aligns with modern communication demands. The proposed capacity-building program supports administrators in fostering continuous professional development for teachers.

Parents. Being the primary advocates for their children's education, are integral to the educational process. Parents benefit from a clearer understanding of the educational strategies being employed in their child's learning environment. This knowledge empowers parents to actively support their children's education at home, fostering a collaborative learning environment.

Researcher. As a pioneer in the pursuit of knowledge, the researcher stands to gain substantial benefits from this study. Delving into this research offers a valuable foundation for the researcher's future academic exploration and investigation. The study provides a foundational understanding of the impact of multi-modal literacy in Filipino education. The researcher can build upon this foundation to conduct further studies, exploring nuances, variations, and potential improvements in multi-modal literacy strategies.

Future Researchers. The findings contribute to educational theory by expanding the understanding of effective literacy practices. This benefits future researchers and scholars interested in literacy, communication, and educational psychology.

Chapter 2

REVIEW OF RELATED LITERATURE AND STUDIES

This chapter presents the literature and studies relevant to the research tasked that are consequent from the dissertations, books and other reference materials. This chapter also shows the gaps to be linked, synthesis of the study, the theoretical and conceptual frameworks. The last section of this chapter presents the effective definitions of key terms used in the study.

A multimodal text uses two or more modes to do this. Every mode generates meaning using distinct semiotic resources. A poster, for instance, uses written language, still images, and spatial design to communicate meaning. Multimodality can be paper-based, live, or digital; multimodality does not always imply the use of technology. Graphic novels, comics, picture books, textbooks, and posters are examples of paper-based multimodal texts. Live multimodal texts, like dance, performance, and oral storytelling, use a variety of modes, including gestural, spatial, auditory, and oral language, to convey meaning. Film, animation, slide shows, e-posters, digital stories, podcasts, and web pages with hyperlinks to external translations or pronunciation guides are examples of digital multimodal texts (Victoria State Government, n.d.).

The significance of teaching multimodal literacy is for modern communication to be effective; youth must be able to understand, react to, and create meaning from multimodal texts in a variety of formats. Multimodal literacy refers to the ability to comprehend, create, and critically analyze meaning conveyed through a combination of modes. These modes can include written language, images, audio, video, and spatial design. This stands in stark contrast to traditional literacy, which focuses primarily on proficiency in written language. In order to accomplish this, it is imperative that students receive explicit instruction on how each mode employs distinct semiotic resources to communicate meaning (Kress, 2010).

In written language, this meaning would be conveyed through sentences using noun groups and adjectives typed or written on paper or a screen, whereas the representation of people, objects, and places can be conveyed using choices of visual semiotic resources like line, shape, size, line, and symbols (Callow, 2023) wrote or typed on paper or a screen. In addition, teachers must explain to students how authors switch between modes to choose the best one in which to tell their story and how meaning is "orchestrated" in multimodal texts by choosing and combining different modes in different ways (Jewitt, 2009. p.15). The need to redefine literacy is being highlighted by the way new technologies are transforming the landscape of communication. According to Kress (2003), "human, cognitive/affective, cultural, and bodily engagement with the world and on the forms and shapes of knowledge" will be essential components of literacy in the new media era. He suggests moving away from alphabetic literacy and investigating the new kinds of literacy that are required in the modern world.

These days, being able to communicate effectively across multiple media is a requirement for being deemed literate. The realization that language is typically used in conjunction with other semiotic resources and that meaning is created multimodally as a result of the coordination of these resources is known as the "multimodal turn" (Jewitt, 2009) It is now believed that language is "part of complex sets of interconnecting forms of human semiosis, rather than as some discreetly independent entity" (Christie, 2002). In addition to using language, multimodal resources like pictures, videos, embodied action, and threedimensional objects are also used in communication, particularly when utilizing multimedia and social media, to create meaning in various contexts (Smith et al. 2014).

The 21st century has ushered in a dramatic transformation of communication, driven by the ever-present influence of technology. This necessitates a shift in pedagogical approaches within Filipino classrooms. This study explores the integration of multimodal literacy and global citizenship education (GCE) as a way to equip students with the skills they need to thrive in this new era.

According to Lim and Hung (2016), students must thus acquire complementary competencies in addition to the traditional domains of literacy and numeracy, which are still fundamental. They also need to become fluent in multimodal literacy. Given this, the current literacy curriculum cannot continue to be primarily language-focused. The literacy curriculum needs to change from teaching and learning how to read print to teaching students how to read both print and screen; from reading books to teaching students how to read books and critically view multimodal texts; from writing to typing; and from speaking to speaking and representing. An article by Lim (2018) explains how a pedagogical approach based on systemic functional theory was developed to help Singaporean secondary school students acquire multimodal literacy.

The approach's pedagogical components are in line with the Learning by Design framework, which is popular in the multiliteracies field. The article also describes the systemic functional approach pilot trial that involved two teachers and two classes. The experiment was successful in improving the systemic functional approach for teaching students multimodal literacy. Together, the teachers and the instructional content developers found and selected pertinent lesson materials, such as illustrations of visual texts that would be engaging for the students. Together with the teachers, the pedagogical aspects of the approach were discussed and worked out to fit within the tight parameters of the curriculum.

The meta-language to be introduced through the approach was carefully considered, discussed, and, if feasible, aligned with terms already used in language instruction to ensure that each new term was useful and necessary for the students to use for their description and discussion of multimodal texts. This helped to prevent an overload of terminology. Multimodal grammar instruction for secondary school students can be challenging, it must be acknowledged.

Therefore, we have decided not to introduce visual transitivity at this time after consulting and negotiating with the teachers about the extent of meta-language to be used. Comparatively speaking to ideational and textual meanings made multimodally, interpersonal meanings received more attention. Nevertheless, by going over the media tactics utilized to realize them in a print ad, we have tried to present the fundamental concepts of salience and information value.

The article details the resources created and implemented in a pilot study to instruct students in multimodal literacy. The trial's encouraging results confirm that multimodal literacy can be taught and that designing for its learning can be accomplished through the systemic functional approach outlined in this article. The literacy curriculum needs to be expanded to include multimodal literacy in light of the evolving communicative landscape that our students now live in and the need to provide them with the literacy necessary to understand and create multimodal texts. Teachers are the ones on the front lines of preparing our students for multimodal literacy in the classroom, so they need support from theoretically grounded instructional strategies. Developments in the multimodality field offer rich insights that may find their way into classroom instruction. An attempt to convert these ideas into a teaching strategy for multimodal literacy is represented by the systemic functional approach discussed in this article.

In the educational system, the effective development of a student's skills is highly valued and given importance, particularly in language learning and engagement in communication. Proficiency in the five macro skills is considered a necessity for successful language and communication learning. The macro skills referred to are listening, speaking, reading, writing, and viewing, each with its own set of communication rules in a specified context. Each of these skills can open doors to various cultures and knowledge in society. Therefore, a student equipped with sufficient knowledge in the five macro skills is deemed empowered and successful in any field they choose to pursue. It emphasized the continuous search for ways to learn the principles of these macro skills, which leads to successful communication and personal development. This simply implies that a student who has mastered scholarly listening, speaking, reading, writing, and viewing is prepared for any academic challenge that may arise.

Due to the rapid advancement of technology, multimedia is considered an innovation in the concept of learning and is utilized in various subjects such as Filipino. Indeed, it creates numerous opportunities, especially in learning, as it combines internal knowledge and diverse representations to integrate texts, videos, images, and other interactive learning tools. Therefore, students need to understand that watching multimedia is not just for entertainment but is relevant to their studies, so it should be used appropriately. The use of multimedia in the classroom should be intrinsic and contextually linked to the lesson. Thus, its integration into the curriculum requires a balance between the overall content of what students observe and other aspects they perceive from it. The video can be considered a narrator with multiple meanings, and viewers can provide various interpretations.

The rapid advancement of technology has fundamentally altered communication practices, with multimedia becoming an integral part of daily life. This is reflected in the educational context, where Filipino teachers are increasingly incorporating multimedia resources into their curriculum.

In response to the modern teaching system for the 21st century, Filipino teachers need a contemporary strategy related to multimodal methods to ensure the equitable development of a student's capabilities. The changes in the classroom curriculum pose a significant challenge for teachers to keep up with the current classroom system. As mentioned by Olayinka (2016), students exposed to appropriate learning methods demonstrate more concrete abilities compared to those who learned in a traditional classroom setting. (Pungtilan, 2022)

The integration of multi-modal literacy and global citizenship education (GCE) within Filipino classrooms is underpinned by several key studies. Jewitt (2008) emphasizes the importance of incorporating various modes of communication—visual, auditory, and textual—in classrooms to cater to different learning styles, highlighting a shift from traditional literacy to a more inclusive approach. Cope and Kalantzis (2009) discuss multiliteracies, stressing the ability to interpret and create meaning through diverse modes, which is crucial for Filipino teachers. Kress (2010) provides a social semiotic approach to multimodality, offering theoretical foundations for analyzing and improving multimodal literacy practices among teachers.

This study can benefit from including "Teaching Critical Literacy Using Multimodal Texts to College Students in the Philippines" by Margarita Felipe Fajardo within its review of relevant literature. Fajardo's research directly tackles multimodal literacy, a core theme of the investigation. An analysis of her findings can offer valuable insights into Filipino teachers' current understanding and potential hurdles when incorporating these types of texts into their curriculum.

Although the research targets college students, it emphasizes the importance of equipping educators with the necessary skills to navigate and teach using multimodal resources. Furthermore, Fajardo's study focuses specifically on the Philippine context, providing crucial information about the current state of literacy practices within the country. By incorporating this related literature, the study can establish a stronger foundation by demonstrating an understanding of the specific needs the proposed capacity building program aims to address.(University of Wollongong, 2016).

The integration of multimodal learning spaces and literacy frameworks in teaching deaf students is an evolving field, particularly significant in the context of

Filipino education. Research by Francisco, Sulse, and Wang (2023) underscores the effectiveness of multimodal learning spaces in enhancing literacy among Filipino deaf students by employing visual aids, sign language, written texts, and digital tools. This comprehensive framework focuses on visual literacy, digital literacy, and collaborative learning, ensuring that literacy instruction is both accessible and engaging. These approaches align with global best practices advocated by the American Annals of the Deaf, which emphasize the use of technology and multimodal strategies to improve literacy instruction.

Moreover, in accordance to the research of Francisco, M.P.B.U., Sulse, L.D., & Wang, Y. (2024), studies on Filipino teachers' practices in multimodal literacy and global citizenship education reveal a trend towards adopting these multimodal approaches to cater to diverse student needs. Key practices include the use of technology, collaborative projects, and differentiated instruction, which collectively aim to enhance academic performance and prepare students for global participation. Despite the promising potential, significant challenges such as resource limitations, inadequate teacher training, and the need for comprehensive curriculum development persist.

To address these challenges, according to Francisco, M.P.B.U., Sulse, L.D., & Wang, Y. (2024) the literature recommends investing in technological resources, implementing ongoing professional development for teachers, and creating collaborative networks to share best practices. A structured capacity-building program for teachers is essential to equip them with the skills and knowledge necessary to effectively integrate multimodal strategies into their classrooms. By overcoming these challenges, the potential of multimodal learning spaces in improving literacy education for Filipino deaf students can be fully realized.

Multimodal literacies encompass a range of literate practices integrating multiple modes of communication, such as visual, auditory, spatial, and linguistic modes, aligning with the dynamic ways students interact with texts in the digital age. The critical review by Tan, Zammit, D'warte, and Gearside (2020) highlights the importance of embracing diverse modalities, including visual, digital, and performative texts, to recognize students' diverse literacies beyond traditional reading and writing. They emphasize the need for innovative pedagogical strategies and holistic, flexible assessment practices that consider the complexity of multimodal compositions, advocating for equitable access to resources to bridge the digital divide. In a study focusing on Filipino teachers' practices, the integration of multimodal literacies with global citizenship education is recognized as essential for fostering students' understanding and empathy towards global issues.

This study identifies significant professional development needs to equip teachers with the skills to integrate multimodal literacies effectively, despite challenges such as limited access to technology and insufficient systemic support.

Furthermore, the American Annals of the Deaf highlights the critical role of visual literacies and inclusive pedagogical practices in deaf education, emphasizing the need for assessment adaptations to accommodate multimodal literacies (Author(s), year). Overall, the implementation of multimodal literacies enhances students' critical thinking, creativity, and global citizenship, requiring comprehensive professional development, equitable resource access, and inclusive assessment practices to prepare students for modern challenges. Research by Francisco, Sulse, and Wang (2023) offers promising insights into the effectiveness of multimodal learning spaces for Filipino deaf students. This approach combines visual aids, sign language, written texts, and digital tools to create an accessible and engaging learning environment. It aligns with global best practices advocated Research by Ryan Bernido Network (2022) highlights the proactive approach taken by the Philippines in addressing the needs of diverse learners through programs like the Indigenous Education Program (IPEd). These initiatives recognize the value of students' home languages and cultures, fostering a sense of identity and belonging within the classroom. Additionally, the emphasis on culture-based education practices, such as teacher training for IPEd and contextualized lesson plans, lays a strong foundation for the development of multilingual literacies.

The educational landscape in the Philippines is undergoing a significant transformation. This is driven by several factors, including the increasing prevalence of technology, the evolving nature of communication, and the recognition of the need to prepare students for success in a globalized world. This research explores two key areas that can contribute to this transformation: integrating multimodal learning spaces and fostering global citizenship education (GCE) within Filipino classrooms.

Multicultural literacy is the skill of looking for and gaining knowledge without regard to cultural prejudices. It is also the capacity to acknowledge the diversity of perspectives in order to a more sympathetic evaluation of any circumstance. It is significant for both the present and upcoming student generations to possess multicultural knowledge, given that Phillippines is extremely multicultural. Pupils must be able to consider the opinions of various cultures in order to enable themselves to develop as responsible citizens who consider the perspectives of other's viewpoints.

Multicultural literature, or literature with elements from many cultures, is an effective tool for helping students understand other people's cultures as well as their own. Relationships between students from different cultural backgrounds can be strengthened and gaps between them can be filled with this deeper knowledge. Even if they decide not to travel abroad, students in the twenty-first century must develop cultural sensitivity because they are global citizens.

Studies have indicated that students' comprehension of contemporary global issues is enhanced when they can connect global events to the themes, contradictions, and characterizations found in multicultural literature. Thus, as they learn to interact with and evaluate texts critically, students develop stronger reasoning abilities.

Students who read multicultural literature are less likely to feel alienated from one another and have higher self-esteem. It has the capacity to foster acceptance, empathy, and respect in every student. In order to help students understand that all children have the same emotions regardless of where they live on the planet, what language they speak, or how they appear, we should introduce them to books that highlight human similarities rather than differences. These novels show that despite people's great differences, there are a lot of things in common that can bring people together. Narratives that highlight cultural diversity can foster the belief that race is not a barrier but rather a feature of our multicultural world (Kaitharath, 2020).

Multicultural education lacks a singular definition, as it can be interpreted from various perspectives. Nevertheless, it can be described as the incorporation of cultural awareness from diverse ethnic groups into education, seen as an unavoidable outcome of the social reality in Western countries (Geng, 2013). Sherpa (2019) asserts that all students, irrespective of gender, social class, or ethnic, racial, and cultural characteristics, should have equal learning opportunities. This is crucial because of the diverse types of learners in society. Geng (2013) explores multicultural education in China within the context of globalization, highlighting its different connotations and roots in Western countries. Geng emphasizes that multicultural education emerged primarily in the United States, addressing the education challenges of minority ethnic groups to alleviate contradictions and conflicts between multiple nationalities. Despite criticisms suggesting that multicultural education may perpetuate racialism or hinder students' basic capacities, some scholars, including Sherpa (2019), see it as a solution to educational problems in diverse societies. Sherpa (2019) extensively reviews multicultural education, linking it to Nepal as a country with diverse ethnicities. Multicultural education, according to Sherpa, draws from various cultures, embedding indigenous thoughts to create new knowledge and promote equal value and appreciation within the culture.

The necessity for multicultural education is underscored by the need for ethnically and culturally literate citizens, respect for human beings and dignity, globalization of education, and the development of new skills. Teachers play a crucial role in achieving a successful multicultural education system, requiring a basic understanding of multicultural education, initiative in incorporating cultural diversity in teaching, and the capacity for critical analysis (Geng, 2013).

Sherpa (2019) emphasizes that multicultural education is responsive to different types of learners. In the Philippines, multicultural education aligns with the country's inclusive education initiatives. DepEd Order No. 72 (2009) and the Enhanced Basic Education Act of 2013 define inclusive education as accepting all children, including those with disabilities or under difficult circumstances. In the Philippines, where various sub-groups with distinct beliefs and cultures exist, the implementation of a multicultural education system is essential.

The Philippines, although not yet highly diverse in terms of races or nationalities, is proactive in addressing the needs of different learners. Programs like the Indigenous Education Program (IPEd) and other inclusive education initiatives cater to diverse groups. The government's responsiveness lays the groundwork for a successful multicultural education system in the future when the country becomes more populated by different races. The implementation of culture-based education practices, such as teacher training for IPEd and contextualized lesson plans, is a positive step toward achieving multicultural education (Ryan Bernido Network, 2022)

Multicultural literacy equips students with the skills to understand and appreciate diverse perspectives. Through exposure to multicultural literature, students develop empathy, respect, and a sense of global citizenship (Kaitharath, 2020). Studies by Geng (2013) and Sherpa (2019) explore the concept of multicultural education, highlighting its importance in fostering inclusive learning environments that cater to the diverse needs of students in the Philippines. This aligns with the country's existing initiatives for inclusive education, as outlined in DepEd Order No. 72 (2009) and the Enhanced Basic Education Act of 2013.

However, the implementation of multicultural education goes beyond simply including diverse literature in the curriculum. Teachers play a critical role in facilitating discussions that encourage students to critically analyze cultural perspectives and recognize the interconnectedness of the world. This requires ongoing professional development opportunities that equip educators with the necessary pedagogical skills and cultural sensitivity to effectively guide these discussions (Geng, 2013).

Furthermore, fostering multicultural literacy extends beyond classroom walls. Encouraging students to engage with diverse communities through service learning projects or cultural exchange programs can deepen their understanding and appreciation of different perspectives. These experiences can also help students develop critical thinking skills as they grapple with complex global issues like social justice, environmental sustainability, and human rights.

According to García & Flores (2013), certain academics advocate for the term "multilingual literacies" to underscore the presence of not only two but various languages and literacies. This term encompasses the diversity of individual and group repertoires, highlighting the myriad ways in which individuals utilize and blend codes within their communicative range.

In addition, educators are increasingly operating in multilingual classrooms where students employ various languages in their language practices. As demonstrated in their work, literacy extends beyond mere reading and writing skills. Literacy practices are intricately linked to and influenced by social, cultural, political, and economic factors, involving intricate social interactions. Therefore, the approach to teaching literacy in multilingual classrooms must shift towards a versatile, multi-faceted model of pluriliteracies. In this model, students are encouraged by the teacher, even if she is monolingual, to incorporate all their home and community language practices to comprehend the school text. This approach enables students to effectively engage with texts in an additional language, enhancing their identity investment. Consequently, they develop the pluriliteracies crucial in our globally connected 21st-century world.

The concept of multilingual literacies, as explored by García & Flores (2013), emphasizes the importance of acknowledging and integrating the diverse language skills that students bring to the classroom. This approach recognizes the complex ways individuals utilize and blend languages within their communication practices. In the context of the Philippines, where various languages and dialects coexist, promoting multilingual literacies becomes even more crucial.

The paper concludes with recommendations for further study and suggestions for policymakers. The debate surrounding MTB-MLE, since its inception, revolves around proponents advocating for equal educational opportunities for all children and opponents expressing concerns about its potential long-term effects, particularly in a globalized world where English serves as the lingua franca. Education is a crucial factor for success in life, but the evolving landscape of globalization has altered the dynamics, making proficiency in English equally essential for success on a global scale.

The implementation of Mother Tongue-Based Multilingual Education (MTB-MLE) in the Philippines has raised concerns about its potential impact on the English literacy development of Filipino children. This paper delves into an experimental study conducted by Namanya (2017), where pre-tests and posttests were administered to two groups of 68 students from a public elementary school in Silang, Philippines. One group was instructed in the mother tongue, while the other was taught in English. The test results, analyzed using t-tests through the Statistical Package for Social Sciences (SPSS), revealed a decline in English literacy levels among children taught in the mother tongue, supporting certain language acquisition theories and scholars' concerns.

The experimental study's findings indicate that MTB-MLE may indeed have adverse effects on children's English literacy, jeopardizing their competitiveness in the global arena. However, the study has certain limitations. Firstly, the treatment duration was short, spanning only about two weeks. Secondly, the sample size of 68 Grade 3 students is relatively small compared to the school's overall population of approximately 960 students under the MTB-MLE program. To address these limitations, it is recommended that similar studies be conducted with larger sample sizes and extended treatment durations, ideally covering an entire school year. Additionally, research in different settings with participants from various language groups would contribute to a more comprehensive understanding. Further studies should also assess how countries implementing MTB-MLE perform on the global stage. Periodic evaluations by the government are essential to ensure that the policy aligns with its intended purpose. Ultimately, the government should prioritize and implement a language-in-education policy that effectively addresses the nation's top priorities.

In terms of GCE, Banks (2008) underscores the role of education in promoting global citizenship by developing students' awareness of global issues and cultural diversity. UNESCO's (2015) guide outlines practical strategies for integrating GCE into lessons, providing essential themes and learning objectives.

Oxley and Morris (2013) offer a typology of global citizenship, categorizing different pedagogical strategies and helping teachers understand various GCE approaches.

Focusing on the Filipino context, Bernardo (2014) examines the integration of intercultural understanding and GCE in the Philippine education system, identifying challenges and opportunities for teachers. Pooten and Amorado (2015) investigate the current practices of Filipino teachers in GCE, highlighting barriers and areas needing capacity building. Mendoza (2018) focuses on how Filipino teachers perceive and practice multiliteracies in their classrooms, providing empirical data on the effectiveness of multi-modal literacy strategies.

For capacity building, Guskey (2002) outlines the key components of effective professional development programs, emphasizing ongoing support and practical application. Avalos (2011) reviews trends and best practices in teacher professional development, offering insights for creating robust programs. DarlingHammond, Hyler, and Gardner (2017) identify features of effective professional development, such as content focus, active learning, and collaboration, which are crucial for developing a successful capacity building program for multi-modal literacy and GCE. These studies collectively provide a comprehensive foundation for understanding and enhancing the practices of Filipino teachers in multi-modal literacy and GCE.

As stated by Itaas, E. (2011). Capacity-building for Philippine Public Secondary School Teachers on Information and Communications Technology Literacy Training Program. Itaas' study delves into the realm of capacity-building initiatives tailored specifically for Philippine public secondary school teachers, focusing on Information and Communications Technology (ICT) literacy training. This research is particularly relevant as it explores avenues to enhance educators' competencies in utilizing digital tools and resources, a crucial aspect in today's technologically driven educational landscape. By examining the effectiveness of such training programs, Itaas sheds light on strategies to empower teachers with the skills necessary to integrate ICT into various instructional contexts.

This literature contributes valuable insights to the broader discourse on capacity-building for educators in the Philippines, complementing the proposed program aimed at enhancing teachers' practices in multi-modal literacy and global citizenship education.

As per Kumari, S. (2022). Teacher's Views on Training and Capacity Building in Education. [Insert publication details]. Kumari's study delves into the perspectives of teachers regarding training and capacity building in education, offering valuable insights into their professional development needs and preferences. By examining teachers' views on various training modalities, including workshops, seminars, and in-service programs, Kumari sheds light on the effectiveness of different approaches in enhancing educators' competencies and instructional practices. This research is particularly relevant as it provides firsthand perspectives from teachers, which can inform the design and implementation of capacity-building initiatives tailored to their specific needs and preferences. By incorporating the findings of Kumari's study, the proposed capacity-building program for Filipino teachers can be further refined to ensure alignment with teachers' views and aspirations, ultimately enhancing its impact and effectiveness in promoting multi-modal literacy and global citizenship education.

According to Ines (2023), Philippines ranked 77th out of 81 countries globally in the recent student assessment conducted by the Organization for Economic Co-operation and Development (OECD) for 15-year-old learners. The results of the Programme for International Student Assessment (PISA) 2022 revealed that the Philippines once again performed poorly in reading, mathematics, and science, falling below the OECD average in all three subjects. In reading literacy, although there was a marginal improvement in scores from 2018, with an average of 347 points in 2022, the Philippines still lagged far behind the global average of 476 points.

The OECD suggested that policymakers and educators in the Philippines learn from the policies and practices of other countries to address these educational challenges. Former Department of Education (DepEd) Secretary Leonor Briones expressed hope for improvement in the Philippines' performance in the 2022 PISA assessment, but the current DepEd leadership tempered expectations, indicating that high scores were not anticipated. In response to the findings, the DepEd initiated the National Learning

Recovery Program (NLRP) aimed at enhancing students' reading, math, and science skills. This program seeks to close learning gaps and support K to 12 learners in achieving learning standards across public elementary and secondary schools nationwide. Overall, the results of the PISA 2022 assessment highlight the urgent need for reforms and interventions to improve the quality of education in the Philippines, particularly in mathematics, reading, and science, in order to better equip Filipino students for success in the global arena.

Furthermore, According to Lucat et al. (2021) In the 2018 Programme for International Student Assessment (PISA), Filipino 15-year-old students ranked last globally in reading proficiency, with only 19% meeting the minimum standard. This underscores the need to understand the factors contributing to their low reading proficiency and to implement effective interventions to address this issue. A study utilizing machine learning methods was conducted to identify variables predictive of low reading proficiency among Filipino students using Philippine PISA data. The analysis identified 20 variables associated with low reading proficiency, reflecting aspects of students' psychosocial experiences at home, in the classroom, and within the school environment. These variables encompassed beliefs, motivations, experiences, and resources that distinguish students with low reading proficiency from their peers.

The study used data from 7,233 15-year-old Filipino students from the OECD PISA 2018 database. Stratified sampling was employed to select schools and students from different regions of the Philippines. Students were categorized into low and high reading proficiency groups based on their performance levels. The analysis revealed three interrelated social environments or contexts—socioeconomic, classroom, and school social—that strongly influenced students' poor reading performance.

Firstly, by Francisco, M.P.B.U., Sulse, L.D., & Wang, Y. (2024) socioeconomic factors such as low socioeconomic status (SES) were associated with limited access to resources like ICT at home, affecting students' engagement and motivation to learn. Secondly, classroom experiences, including teacher feedback and lack of enthusiasm, impacted students' self-concept and intrinsic motivation to read. Lastly, negative experiences within the school social environment, such as social disconnection and exposure to bullying, hindered students' attitude towards learning and holistic development.

In conclusion, the study identified non-cognitive variables beyond traditional educational targets that influence Filipino students' reading proficiency. Interventions should address these variables, focusing on improving students' psychosocial experiences in school. Additionally, interventions need to be contextualized and localized to accommodate diverse school and community settings.

Reading comprehension entails the ability to decipher individual words and extract profound meaning from the information presented orally or in writing. It holds significant importance in the overall functioning of a society and serves as a foundational element of literacy. In a study by Caraig and Quimbo (2022) that aims to evaluate the level of reading comprehension among Senior High School students in their Core Science Subjects and identify various factors influencing individuals' reading comprehension abilities. Using a descriptive survey approach, the study determines the distribution and range of certain social characteristics, such as educational background, occupation, and geographical location, and explore their potential correlation with specific behavioral patterns or attitudes. The assessment tools for reading comprehension include stories of varying difficulty levels: Upper Beginner, Intermediate, and Upper Intermediate.

Students who achieve a correct answer rate of 75% or higher are classified as "mastery level," while those scoring between 50% and 74% are considered "near mastery level." Students scoring below 50% are categorized as "low mastery level," following Imam's (2014) reader categorization criteria.

The findings reveal that only a mere 7% of the total respondents' exhibit mastery level reading comprehension skills. This percentage is notably low compared to the 49% classified as near mastery level and the remaining 44% categorized as poor mastery level readers. The results shows a lot about the current state of the learner's reading comprehension and it is a well-known problem that's why there are a lot of programs being implemented by the government in order to help these students. One of those is the "Catch Up Fridays," a new program aimed at addressing the pervasive issue of poor reading comprehension skills among Filipino students. Recognizing the pressing need for intervention, teachers were tasked with dedicating half of the day to activities such as reading clubs and read-aloud sessions. However, the urgency of the situation was underscored by University of the Philippines (UP) College of Education professor Portia Padilla, who emphasized the critical importance of high-quality reading instruction for the success of such initiatives.

According to Professor Portia Padilla of University of the Philippines (UP) College of Education she had highlighted a significant concern: not all teachers possessed the necessary competencies to effectively teach reading. Studies had revealed that a considerable number of elementary school teachers struggled with basic reading skills themselves. Despite previous efforts by the Department of

Education, such as a reading program in the Bangsamoro region, the inadequacy of teacher training had remained a persistent obstacle. The gravity of the situation was further emphasized by Padilla's questioning of the readiness of teachers to provide remedial learning on Fridays, given that nine out of ten students grappled with reading difficulties. It was clear that a mere introduction of programs like "Catch Up Fridays" was insufficient without a comprehensive strategy to equip teachers with the requisite knowledge and skills for effective reading instruction. The urgency of the matter was not lost on lawmakers either, who recognized the imperative to enhance teacher education in response to consistently low passing rates in the Licensure Exam for Teachers (LET). However, the challenges persisted: overcrowded classrooms, limited reading materials, and overburdened teachers continued to hinder progress in addressing the literacy crisis. Underscored by Professor Portia Padilla Padilla of University of the Philippines (UP) College of Education.

Senator Sherwin Gatchalian, who chaired the Committee on Basic Education, emphasized the urgent need for programs and interventions to enhance reading proficiency among Filipino students, especially in light of the exacerbation of educational challenges by the pandemic. He declared the National Book Week from November 24 to 30 that is celebrated in 2022 amid the ongoing struggle to address the declining reading proficiency of Filipino learners. Even before the pandemic, according to Senator Gatchalian the international assessments had revealed that Filipino learners were already facing difficulties in meeting the minimum proficiency standards in reading. The Philippines scored lowest in Reading out of 79 countries in the 2018 Programme for International Student Assessment (PISA), with only one in five 15-year-old Filipino learners achieving at least the minimum proficiency level in Overall Reading Literacy. Additionally, the 2019 Southeast Asia Primary Learning Metrics reported that only 10 percent of Grade 5 learners in the Philippines reached the minimum proficiency level at the end of primary education. Moreover, the World Bank estimated that learning poverty in the Philippines stood at 90.9 percent as of June, indicating the high percentage of 10-year-old children who struggled to read or comprehend simple stories.

Senator Gatchalian proposed Senate Bill 150, known as the Academic Recovery and Accessible Learning (ARAL) Act, which aims to establish a nationwide learning recovery program. This program would include structured tutorial sessions and remediation plans, with a priority on developing critical and analytical thinking skills through reading. Furthermore, he proposed Senate Bill 475 to designate November as National Reading Month, fostering a culture of reading among basic education learners and their communities through nationwide programs and activities.

During the Annual National Congress of the Philippine Librarians Association, Inc. in Iloilo City on November 23, Vice President and Department of Education Sara Duterte emphasized the essential role of librarians and access to public libraries in addressing learning loss and insurgency. She highlighted the importance of addressing literacy as a crucial aspect of post-pandemic learning recovery, emphasizing the roles of both parents and teachers in promoting reading comprehension among learners.

The National Book Week celebration, led by the librarians' association, National Library of the Philippines, and National Commission for Culture and the Arts - National Committee on

Libraries and Information Services, carried the theme "Basa, Bayan, Bukas" (read, country, for the future). This theme reflects the collective effort to promote reading and literacy as essential elements for the country's future development and prosperity.

In conclusion, the dire state of reading comprehension skills among Filipino students necessitated immediate and concerted action. The implementation of reading programs like “Catch Up Fridays” was a step in the right direction, but it underscored the pressing need for sustained investment in teacher training and resources to ensure the effectiveness of such initiatives. Without addressing the root causes of the problem and adequately supporting educators, the goal of improving literacy levels would remain elusive.

A mixed-method research by Tomas et al. (2021) was carried out to explore the reading profiles, challenges, and lessons learned regarding English and Filipino reading among learners, alongside schools' agendas and initiatives aimed at enhancing reading programs to address these challenges. A total of 4,056 Filipino reading profiles and 4216 English reading profiles from Grade 1 to Grade 7 students were analyzed, along with interview responses from school heads and teachers, using descriptive measures and thematic analysis.

The findings revealed by Tomas et al (2021) that a significant majority of learners were operating at the frustration level in both English and Filipino reading. Root causes identified included a lack of mastery of reading elements, the presence of at-risk learners, and a deficient reading culture.

Proposed solutions included the implementation of various reading programs and activities, categorized into Literacy Program, Individual Reading Recovery Program, and Enrichment/Enhancement Program. These initiatives could potentially contribute to the development of contextualized reading curricula and serve as literacy initiatives within schools. In conclusion, the study highlights the pressing need for improving reading levels among learners, given the predominant frustration level observed. The identified causes of reading challenges underscore the importance of addressing fundamental reading skills and fostering a culture of reading. The recommended reading programs and activities offer practical strategies for schools to enhance students' reading abilities. Additionally, it is suggested that similar studies be conducted in other school divisions to inform and guide the development of contextualized reading initiatives tailored to specific educational contexts.

According to Ines (2023), Philippines ranked 77th out of 81 countries globally in the recent student assessment conducted by the Organization for Economic Co-operation and Development (OECD) for 15-year-old learners. The results of the Programme for International Student Assessment (PISA) 2022 revealed that the Philippines once again performed poorly in reading, mathematics, and science, falling below the OECD average in all three subjects. In reading literacy, although there was a marginal improvement in scores from 2018, with an average of 347 points in 2022, the Philippines still lagged far behind the global average of 476 points. The OECD suggested that policymakers and educators in the Philippines learn from the policies and practices of other countries to address these educational challenges. Former Department of Education (DepEd) Secretary Leonor Briones expressed hope for improvement in the Philippines' performance in the 2022 PISA assessment, but the current DepEd leadership tempered expectations, indicating that high scores were not anticipated. In response to the findings, the DepEd initiated the National Learning Recovery Program (NLRP) aimed at enhancing students' reading, math, and science skills. This program seeks to close learning gaps and support K to 12 learners in achieving learning standards across public elementary and secondary schools nationwide. Overall, the results of the PISA 2022 assessment highlight the urgent need for reforms and interventions to improve the quality of education in the Philippines, particularly in mathematics, reading, and science, in order to better equip Filipino students for success in the global arena.

Furthermore, According to Lucat et al. (2021) In the 2018 Programme for International Student Assessment (PISA), Filipino 15-year-old students ranked last globally in reading proficiency, with only 19% meeting the minimum standard. This underscores the need to understand the factors contributing to their low reading proficiency and to implement effective interventions to address this issue. A study utilizing machine learning methods was conducted to identify variables predictive of low reading proficiency among Filipino students using Philippine PISA data. The analysis identified 20 variables associated with low reading proficiency, reflecting aspects of students' psychosocial experiences at home, in the classroom, and within the school environment. These variables encompassed beliefs, motivations, experiences, and resources that distinguish students with low reading proficiency from their peers.

Firstly, by Lucat et al. (2021) socioeconomic factors such as low socioeconomic status (SES) were associated with limited access to resources like ICT at home, affecting students' engagement and motivation to learn. Secondly, classroom experiences, including teacher feedback and lack of enthusiasm, impacted students' self-concept and intrinsic motivation to read. Lastly, negative experiences within the school social environment, such as social disconnection and exposure to bullying, hindered students' attitude towards learning and holistic development. In conclusion, the study identified non-cognitive variables beyond traditional educational targets that influence Filipino students' reading proficiency. Interventions should address these variables, focusing on improving students' psychosocial experiences in school. Additionally, interventions need to be contextualized and localized to accommodate diverse school and community settings.

Reading comprehension entails the ability to decipher individual words and extract profound meaning from the information presented orally or in writing. It holds significant importance in the overall functioning of a society and serves as a foundational element of literacy. In a study by Caraig and Quimbo (2022) that aims to evaluate the level of reading comprehension among Senior High School students in their Core Science Subjects and identify various factors influencing individuals' reading comprehension abilities. The assessment tools for reading comprehension include stories of varying difficulty levels: Upper Beginner, Intermediate, and Upper Intermediate. Students who achieve a correct answer rate of 75% or higher are classified as "mastery level," while those scoring between

50% and 74% are considered "near mastery level." Students scoring below 50% are categorized as "low mastery level," following Imam's (2014) reader categorization criteria.

The findings reveal that only a mere 7% of the total respondents' exhibit mastery level reading comprehension skills. This percentage is notably low compared to the 49% classified as near mastery level and the remaining 44% categorized as poor mastery level readers. The results shows a lot about the current state of the learner's reading comprehension and it is a well-known problem that's why there are a lot of programs being implemented by the government in order to help these students. One of those is the "Catch Up Fridays," a new program aimed at addressing the pervasive issue of poor reading comprehension skills among Filipino students. Recognizing the pressing need for intervention, teachers were tasked with dedicating half of the day to activities such as reading clubs and read-aloud sessions. However, the urgency of the situation was underscored by University of the Philippines (UP) College of Education professor Portia Padilla, who emphasized the critical importance of high-quality reading instruction for the success of such initiatives.

Even before the pandemic, international assessments had revealed that Filipino learners were already facing difficulties in meeting the minimum proficiency standards in reading. The Philippines scored lowest in Reading out of 79 countries in the 2018 Programme for International Student Assessment (PISA), with only one in five 15-year-old Filipino learners achieving at least the minimum proficiency level in Overall Reading Literacy. Additionally, the 2019

Southeast Asia Primary Learning Metrics reported that only 10 percent of Grade 5 learners in the Philippines reached the minimum proficiency level at the end of primary education. Moreover, the World Bank estimated that learning poverty in the Philippines stood at 90.9 percent as of June, indicating the high percentage of 10-year-old children who struggled to read or comprehend simple stories.

Synthesis of the Reviewed Studies

Several studies have delved into the extent of multi-modal literacy practices among Filipino teachers, revealing a discernible trend towards integrating digital tools and diverse literacy formats in their teaching. Increasing utilization of multimedia resources such as videos and interactive websites, indicating a positive shift towards multi-modal approaches. However, challenges persist, found that many teachers feel ill-prepared due to a lack of targeted professional development. Despite these obstacles, the positive impact of multi-modal literacy on student engagement and learning outcomes, emphasizing its potential to cater to diverse learning styles. Identified barriers such as limited access to resources and technical support, underscoring the need for improved infrastructure.

Collectively, these studies highlight both the progress made and the ongoing challenges in promoting multi-modal literacy among Filipino teachers, underscoring the importance of targeted interventions and support mechanisms to foster its widespread adoption in classrooms. The findings laid from the literature sum up to the following ideas are delivered as follows; Filipino teachers' practices regarding multi-modal literacy and global citizenship education (GCE) reveal a growing integration of digital tools and diverse literacy formats in the classroom. However, challenges such as limited access to technology, insufficient training, and resistance to change persist. Similarly, while GCE is being gradually embedded into the curriculum through project-based learning and intercultural exchanges, the lack of a standardized framework and inadequate resources pose significant barriers.

To address these issues, a capacity-building program was proposed, focusing on comprehensive professional development, improved infrastructure, collaborative networks, curriculum integration, and robust monitoring and evaluation. This program aims to equip teachers with the necessary skills and resources to effectively implement multi-modal literacy and GCE, thereby enhancing student engagement and preparing them for global citizenship in a digitally connected world.

Multimodal literacy involves the use of multiple modes, such as written language, images, and spatial design, to convey meaning. This can be paper based, live, or digital, encompassing a variety of formats. Teaching multimodal literacy is crucial in the modern era, where effective communication requires understanding and creating meaning from diverse texts. The curriculum must evolve to teach students how different modes employ distinct semiotic resources. The "multimodal turn" recognizes that language is interconnected with various semiotic resources, and new technologies emphasize the need for expanded literacy beyond traditional language-focused instruction.

Educators play a vital role in preparing students for multimodal literacy. The article discusses a pedagogical approach based on systemic functional theory, aligning with the Learning by Design framework. The approach proved successful in enhancing students' multimodal literacy by carefully selecting engaging lesson materials and incorporating relevant meta-language. Despite challenges in teaching multimodal grammar, the results suggest that effective instruction is possible, emphasizing the need for support and theoretically grounded strategies for teachers. Multicultural literacy involves seeking knowledge without cultural biases, acknowledging diverse perspectives, and fostering empathy. In a multicultural context like the Philippines, students must understand various cultures to become responsible citizens. Multicultural education, incorporating diverse literature and cultural awareness, helps students develop 21st-century skills, critical thinking, and social awareness. The Philippines' inclusive education initiatives align with multicultural education, emphasizing equal learning opportunities for all students. Multilingual literacies recognize the diversity of languages and literacies individuals use in communicative practices. In multilingual classrooms, literacy extends beyond reading and writing skills, involving complex interactions influenced by social, cultural, political, and economic factors. The shift towards pluriliteracies encourages students to incorporate their home and community languages to enhance their identity investment. The paper discusses an experimental study on Mother Tongue-Based Multilingual Education (MTB-MLE) in the Philippines, raising concerns about its impact on English literacy. The findings suggest potential adverse effects on English literacy, prompting recommendations for further studies with larger sample sizes and extended durations. The debate surrounding MTB-MLE emphasizes the importance of aligning language-in-education policies with national priorities.

Theoretical Framework

Pedagogical features in the systemic functional approach to teaching multimodal literacy intricately detail the conceptualization and refinement of a pedagogical framework deeply rooted in systemic functional theory, specifically crafted to advance multimodal literacy among secondary school students in Singapore. The framework's pedagogical features, thoughtfully aligned with the established learning-by-design framework in multiliteracies, underwent a meticulous pilot trial involving collaboration with two teachers across two classes. The outcomes of this trial not only validated the efficacy of the systemic functional approach but also contributed to its nuanced evolution for fostering multimodal literacy.

Throughout the pilot trial, the collaborative effort between educators and researchers focused on developing instructional content that resonated with the unique needs of secondary school students. Teachers played a crucial role in identifying and curating relevant lesson materials, with a specific emphasis on engaging visual texts tailored to captivate student interest. The negotiation of pedagogical features within the constraints of a demanding curriculum was a central aspect, ensuring the practical applicability of the theoretical framework in the classroom setting. A paramount consideration in the development of this approach was the deliberate avoidance of overwhelming students with excessive jargon. The meta-language introduced underwent careful scrutiny, with a concerted effort to align it with existing language teaching terminology. This strategic approach ensured that each introduced term was not only necessary but also conducive to the student's comprehension and articulation of multimodal texts.

Given the inherent complexities of conveying multimodal grammar to secondary school students, the trial strategically focused on interpersonal meanings within the broader context of ideational and textual meanings. Notably, the decision to defer the introduction of visual transitivity showcased a nuanced understanding of the student's cognitive load. The trial also emphasized foundational concepts such as salience and information value, employing practical examples from print advertisements to facilitate comprehension.

The article underscores the positive outcomes of the trial, affirming the teachability of multimodal literacy within the theoretical framework of systemic functional theory. Beyond the pilot trial, the approach underwent iterative refinement and subsequent implementation across various secondary schools in Singapore. The expansion of the framework's scope from print advertisements to films and online news highlights its adaptability and relevance in diverse multimodal contexts.

The evolving nature of this theoretical framework is not confined to the academic realm but extends into practical applications. Workshops were organized to train teachers in Singapore, providing them with the necessary tools to adopt and adapt this theoretical framework in their classrooms.

Inspired by Michael Halliday's call for 'applicable linguistics,' the article positions the development of this theoretical framework as a response to the changing communicative landscape. It underscores the imperative to equip students with the essential literacy skills required to navigate and construct meaning from the diverse array of multimodal texts prevalent in contemporary society. The emphasis on the theoretical grounding of instructional strategies is portrayed as indispensable in supporting teachers, who play a pivotal role in shaping students' multimodal literacy.

Drawing on Kress's assertion about exploring the potentials of representation and communication, the article positions the theoretical framework as a proactive response to the transformative possibilities presented by multimodality. As the educational landscape continues to evolve, the article concludes by advocating for sustained exploration and refinement of theoretical frameworks that adeptly prepare students for the dynamic challenges posed by multimodal communication in the digital age (Lim, 2018).

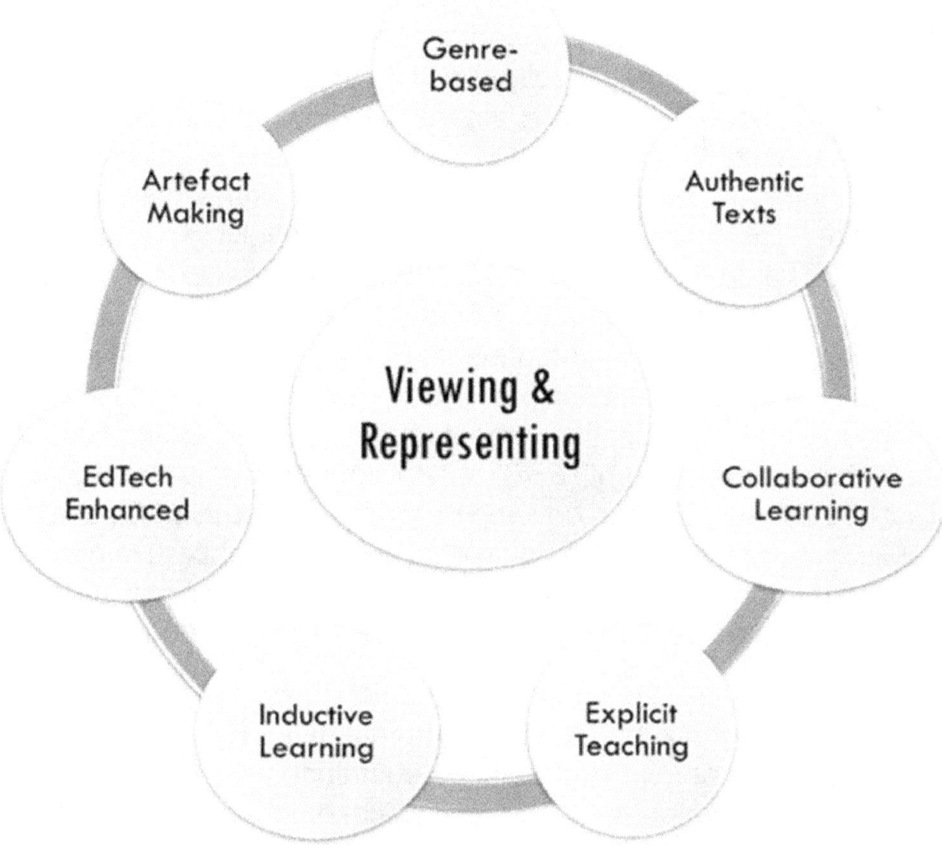

Figure 1: Theoretical Paradigm of the study

Conceptual Framework

The study explores Filipino teachers' practices in multi-modal literacy and global citizenship education (GCE), aiming to develop a capacity-building program based on their needs. Multi-modal literacy refers to the ability to interpret and create texts that combine various modes of communication, such as written, visual, audio, and digital. This concept is grounded in theories such as New Literacy Studies, which focuses on literacy practices as socially situated activities, and the Multi-literacies Framework, emphasizing diverse communication modes and cultural contexts. In the classroom, this involves the use of digital tools, integration of visual, auditory, and kinesthetic learning resources, and project-based learning involving multimedia production. Global Citizenship Education aims to equip learners with the knowledge, skills, and values needed to engage responsibly and effectively in a globally interconnected world. Key theories in GCE include Transformative Learning Theory, which encourages critical reflection and perspective transformation, and Education for Sustainable Development (ESD), integrating principles, values, and practices of sustainable development into education. Classroom practices involve discussions on global issues, collaborative projects with international peers, and the integration of global perspectives and sustainable development goals (SDGs) into the curriculum.

Capacity building focuses on strengthening the abilities of individuals, organizations, and communities to achieve their objectives and improve performance sustainably. Theories such as Professional Development Theory, which emphasizes continuous learning and development for teachers, and Communities of Practice, highlighting collaborative learning among practitioners, guide this component. Strategies for capacity building include workshops, peer mentoring, online courses, and resource-sharing platforms.

The study seeks to answer key questions about current practices in multi-modal literacy and GCE, challenges faced by teachers, and their professional development needs. Data will be collected through surveys, interviews, classroom observations, and focus group discussions. The expected outcomes include a detailed understanding of current practices, identification of challenges and needs, development of a structured capacity-building program, and improved teaching practices that effectively integrate multi-modal literacy and GCE into the curriculum. This conceptual framework provides a structured approach to explore and enhance Filipino teachers' competencies in these critical areas.

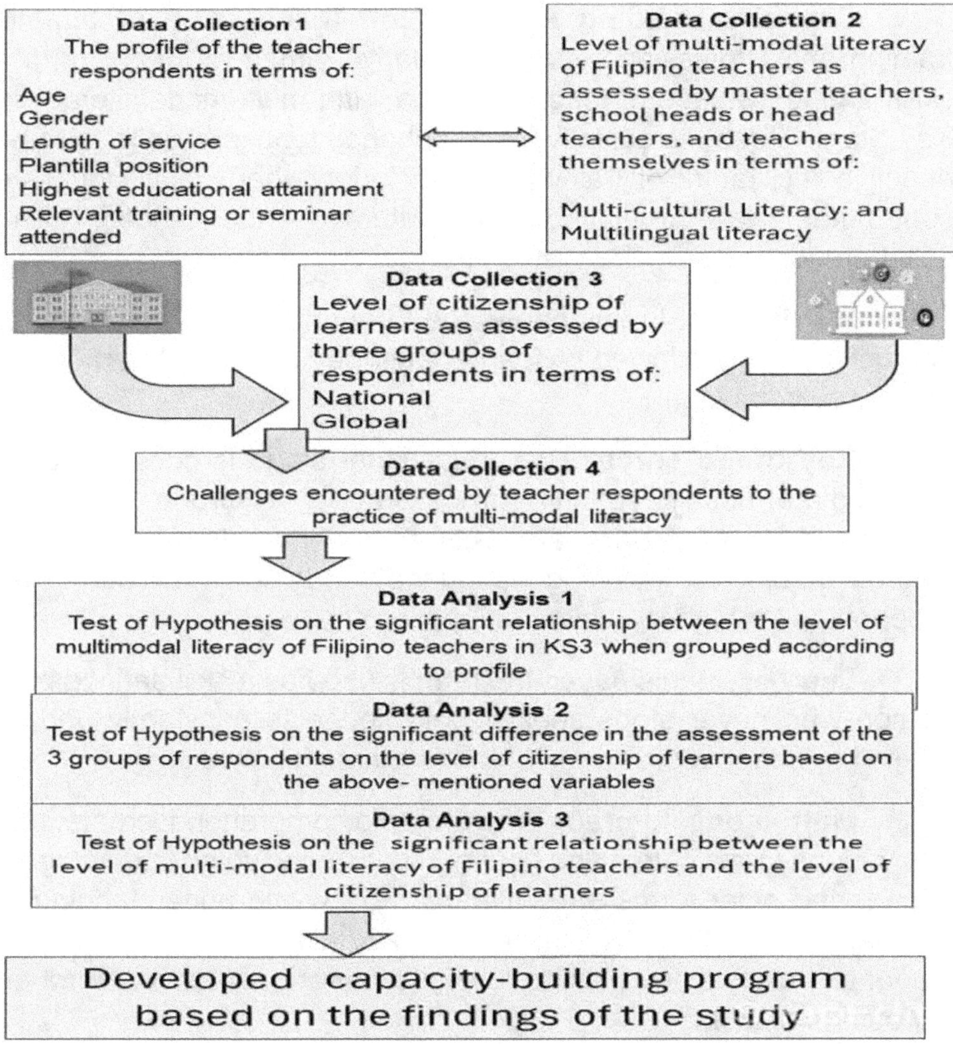

Figure 2. Conceptual Paradigm

Definition of Terms

The following terms are conceptually defined. Some are operationally defined for the researchers to have a better understanding of the relevance of these terms in the present study

Assessment. In this paper, the term is used as the process of judging how much learning has taken place.

Capacity Building Program for Teachers. A systematic training and Professional support initiative aimed at improving the skills and knowledge of teachers in teaching multi-modal literacy in Key Stage Three. Its objective is to enhance teachers' abilities to be effective facilitators of training that includes where multilingualism contributes to enhanced intercultural understanding and collaboration.

Curriculum. In this paper, the term is used as a program of instruction being followed by learners as they go through a mode of training or education.

Key Stage Three. The educational stage is considered as intermediate, usually spanning from Grade 7 to Grade 10, where students are expected to gain in-depth understanding and skills in various subjects, including language and communication, as preparation for higher levels of education.

Learner. In this paper, the term is used as a skill defined by a person who never stops seeking knowledge to constantly update oneself to adapt to the needs of the fast-changing world.

Multi-modal Literacy. The ability to comprehend, create, and use various forms of text and communication, including text, images, sound, and other forms of multimedia, to expand understanding of language and culture. Multi-modal literacy aims to further enhance students' abilities to express their ideas and emotions through various mediums.

National and Global Citizenship. The awareness and understanding of students regarding their role as part of the national community and the broader global society. Its goal is to develop citizens with a profound understanding of culture, history, and issues related to their national existence and engagement in global affairs.

Pedagogical Strategies. In this paper, the term is used as a teaching method that can influence instruction.

School. In this paper, the term is used as an institution where formal learning is conducted.

School Head. In this paper, the term is used as Principal, head teacher, headmistress – the staff member with the greatest responsibility for the management of a school.

Chapter 3

RESEARCH DESIGN AND METHODOLOGY

This part consists of the research design wherein the researcher describes the techniques to be used in this study, the population and sample of the study that specifies the number of respondents; research instrument that explains the tools use in the study.

Research Design

This study employed quantitative descriptive research to determine Filipino Teachers Practices On Multi-Modal Literacy And Global Citizenship Education: Basis For A Proposed Capacity Building Program. Quantitative descriptive research design was defined as an exploratory method that enables researchers to precisely and methodically describe a population, circumstance, or population by which this study sought to conduct the Teachers' readiness for Global Citizenship Knowledge in Key Stage 3.

This study employed the method design which is a quantitative approach to collect and analyze data (Creswell & Tashakkori, 2007). In recent years, quantitative methods have become common in research (Bryman, 2006) because this method design can provide detailed and comprehensive data to achieve the research objectives and answer the research questions.

This study most appropriately employed the explanatory model, which contains quantitative data collection. This method was used to obtain a clearer picture from the quantitative data,

In the explanatory design, the researcher recognized particular quantitative findings that need further explanation.

Also, the researcher utilized a method using survey questionnaires to collect data pertaining behavior of the respondents and analyze the results from the assessment found from the sought answers of the two respondents: Master Teachers / Teachers and, Head Teachers used as the basis for a proposed capacity building program.

Population and Sampling Technique

The study population consisted of all teachers, master teachers and head teachers in the three chosen divisions namely Caloocan, Valenzuela and Manila. A convenient sample of four hundred fifty (450) subjects was selected from the three divisions. The sample included three hundred seventy-five (375) teachers, forty-five (45) master teachers, and thirty (30) head teachers. Available subjects were entered into the study until a sample size of 450 was reached. Subjects who met the sample criteria were identified by the researcher in the three divisions.

The researcher used Slovin's formula to get the number of respondents. Slovin's formula is a statistical method used to determine the appropriate sample size for a survey or study when the population size and desired margin of error are known. The formula is expressed as $n = \frac{N}{1 + N \cdot e^2}$, where n is the sample size, N is the total population size, and e is the margin of error expressed as a decimal.

Research Instrument

In order to have achieved significant data about this study, surveys, and questionnaires gathered quantitative data from teachers about their experiences and practices. Complement with questionnaires, focusing on teachers to explore deeper insights into their instructional strategies, challenges, and professional development needs. This method offered a robust data set to inform the development of an effective capacity-building program a survey questionnaire used as a tool for the respondents to provide accurate and complete information.

The data from the questionnaire were analyzed using descriptive statistics.

Data Gathering Procedure

Prior to the distribution of the questionnaire, there was a personal visit of the researcher to the Schools Division Office of the three different divisions to ask permission to conduct the study with a thorough discussion about how the study is executed. The schedule for the distribution of the questionnaires to the respondents was properly planned and arranged by the researcher through observance of protocol and personal approached in order to get the desired data. The questionnaires were distributed personally and retrieved on the scheduled date.

The researcher also adopted a multi-method approach to ensure the reliability of findings and results. She obtained other means of gathering necessary information to supplement data extracted from the questionnaire. Hence, aside from the approved pre-printed questionnaire, which is utilized for data gathering, the researcher also consulted knowledgeable people or stakeholders.

The researcher exhausted all possible means in gathering the necessary information complemented the data from the sources to ensure a higher degree of reliability, validity, and acceptability.

Statistical Treatment of Data

The data gathered from the respondents were tallied, tabulated, and later analyzed using appropriate statistical tools subject to statistical treatment.

Findings were assessed and evaluated relative to the findings of the other related studies being reviewed to clarify possible similar or contradictory results. The study adopted various statistical tools for correlation and difference of variables under the study.

Adjectival ratings relative to question items corresponding to this study (as presented in the pre-printed, designed questionnaire) scaled every accomplishment of the questionnaire and data analysis.

The statistical tools employed in the study were the following:

1. Frequency and Percentage. The percentage and frequency used to gather information on the profile of the respondents. On the other hand, the percentage was computed by dividing the frequency by the total number of respondents who participated in the survey.
2. Weighted Mean. The mean in each item is to be multiplied by a number (weight) based on the item's relative importance. The resultant aggregate/summation is to be divided by the total number of respondents' z-test. This inferential statistical tool is used to test the null hypothesis. Used in significant testing, it is the value that a test statistic must exceed for the null hypothesis to be rejected.
3. Pearson r. This statistical tool was used to test the null hypothesis. Used in significant testing, it is the value that a test statistic must exceed in order for the null hypothesis to be rejected.
4. Analysis of Variance (ANOVA). This statistical tool is used to test the null hypothesis. Used in significant testing, it is the value that a test statistic must exceed for the null hypothesis to be rejected.

Chapter 4

PRESENTATION, ANALYSIS, AND INTERPRETATION OF DATA

This chapter presents the analysis, interpretation and discussion of the results of gathered information on the multi-modal Literacy in Filipino Teachers Practices towards National and Global Citizenship. Findings are hereby revealed by presenting statistical tables to answer each question presented in the statement of the problems of the study.

1. **Profile of the Teacher Respondents by Frequency and Percentage**

Distribution.

Table 1.1-1.6 presents profile of the teacher Respondents in terms of age, gender, length of service, plantilla position, highest educational attainment, and relevant training or seminar attended.

Table 1. 1 Demographic Profile of the Teachers by Frequency and Percentage Distribution in Terms of **Age**.

Age	Frequency	Percent
21-25 years and below	24	6.40
26-30 years old	22	5.87
31-35 years old	45	12.00
36-40 years old	80	21.33
41-45 years old	95	25.33
46-50 years old	46	12.27
51-55 years old	19	5.60
56-60 years old	44	11.73
Total	**375**	**100**

Table 1.1 presents the frequency and percentage distribution of the profile of the teacher-respondents in terms of age. Age range indicator *41-45 years old* got the highest score frequency of 95 or 25.33%, age range indicator *36-40 years old* got the second highest score frequency of 80 or 21.33%, and age range indicator 4*6-50 years old* got the third highest score frequency 46 or 12.27%. The results show that most teachers are in the prime age of their teaching career. The data was evidently vertically aligned across all age ranges in terms of age maturity in teaching. The data result was in accordance with the data profile of teachers in the Philippines that varies across different regions. Thus, Smith (2020) study found that the majority of novice secondary school teachers in the Philippines were between the ages of 23-29. Another study revealed that the respondents in the study assessing instructional competencies of teachers were mostly in the age range of 31-40 years old. Additionally, a study on student teachers' perceptions found that the respondents belonged to the age group of 19 and above. However, the specific age profile of teachers in the Philippines was not mentioned by the Philippine Statistics Agency.

Table 1.2. Demographic Profile of the Teacher by Frequency and Percentage Distribution in Terms of **Gender.**

Gender	Frequency	Percent
Male	154	41.06
Female	221	58.93
Total	**375**	**100**

Table 1.2 presents the demographic profile through frequency and percentage distribution of the teachers in terms of gender. Gender range indicator *Female* got the highest score frequency of 221or 41.06% followed by gender range indicator *Male* got the second highest score frequency of 154 or 41.06%.

The results revealed that teaching was dominated by female. The findings above further implies the affirmation that the country has a larger number of women teachers than men as supported by the World Bank collection of development indicators in 2020 where 87% of the teachers are women. There is a long-standing debate about whether male or female teachers perform better in the classroom. Research on this topic has produced mixed results, with some studies finding that female teachers are more effective, while others have found no significant difference in the performance of male and female teachers.

Table 1.3. Demographic Profile of the Teachers by Frequency and Percentage Distribution in Terms of **Length on Service in Current Position**

Length on Service in Current Position	**Frequency**	**Percent**
1-5 years	123	32.00
6-10 years	98	26.13
11-15 years	75	20.00
16-20 years	43	11.47
21 and above	36	9.60
Total	**375**	**100**

Table 1.3 presents the frequency and percentage distribution of the profile of the teachers in terms of Length on Service in Current Position . Indicator *1-5 years* got the highest score frequency of 123 or 32.00% Indicator *6-10 years* got the second highest score frequency of 98 or 26.13%, and Indicator *11-15 years* got the third highest score frequency 75 or 20.00%.

The results shows that majority of the respondents were from more than 6 years of teaching of experience. The average teacher has about 15 years of teaching experience. The average teacher has stayed at their current school for eight years. 51% of K-12 teachers in public and private schools have master's degree. 10% have higher than a Master's Degree. Improving teacher quality has become a vital thing to student fulfillment; teacher professionalism gained more prominence. Nowadays, instructors' continuous professional development is broadly visible as crucial for enhancing teachers' overall performance and effectiveness and enhancing dedication to their work. Teachers must always adapt to the current educational system changes to meet the students' needs and demands for the global market. The results also show that majority of the respondents were from more than 6 years of teaching of experience. The average teacher has about 15 years of teaching experience. The average teacher has stayed at their current school for eight years. 51% of K-12 teachers in public and private schools have master's degrees. 10% have higher than a Master's Degree.

Improving teacher quality has become a vital thing to student fulfillment; teacher professionalism gained more prominence. Nowadays, instructors' continuous professional development is broadly visible as crucial for enhancing teachers' overall performance and effectiveness and enhancing dedication to their work.

Table 1.4 Demographic Profile of the Teachers by Frequency and Percentage Distribution in Terms of **Plantilla Position**

Plantilla Position	**Frequency**	**Percent**
Teacher I	182	48.53
Teacher II	123	32.80
Teacher III	70	18.67
Total	**375**	**100**

Table 1.4 presents the frequency and percentage distribution of the profile of the teachers in terms of Plantilla Position. Indicator *Teacher I* got the highest score frequency of 182 or 48.53% Indicator *Teacher II* got the second highest score frequency of 123 or 32.80%, and Indicator *Teacher III* got the third highest score frequency 70 or 18.67%.

The results show that most of the respondents were in Teacher I position. According to DepEd (2021) that in the Philippines, teacher candidates must earn a four-year degree diploma and pass the Board Licensure Exam for Professional

Teachers (BELPT) to be eligible to teach in public schools.

Table 1.5 Demographic Profile of the Teachers by Frequency and

Percentage Distribution in Terms of **Highest Educational Attainment**

Highest Educational Attainment	**Frequency**	**Percent**
Bachelor's Degree	115	30.67
With Units in Master's Degree	103	27.47
Master's Degree	97	25.87
With Units in Doctorate Degree	34	9.06
Doctorate Degree	26	6.53
Total	**375**	**100**

Table 1.5 presents the demographic profile of the teachers by frequency and percentage distribution in terms of Grade Level Assignment. Indicator *Bachelor's Degree* got the highest score frequency of 115 or 30.67%, Indicator *With Units in Master's Degree* got the second highest score frequency of 103 or 27.47%, and

Indicator *Master's Degree* got the third highest score frequency 97 or 25.87%.

The results revealed that most teachers are in the prime age of their teaching career. The data was evidently vertically aligned across all age ranges in terms of age maturity in teaching. According to the respondents observed, the challenges faced by Filipino teachers in their daily work include unpreparedness in teaching multigrade, low allowances, stress, language barrier, classroom management struggles, lack of resources, and lack of support.

The results also show that respondents were equipped in terms of educational attainment. Highest educational attainment refers to the highest grade or year completed in school. The standard teaching credential in the Philippines is a four-year bachelor's degree. Elementary school teachers are qualified through a Bachelor of Elementary Education, and secondary school teachers through a Bachelor of Secondary Education. Public teachers were mostly holder of the degree of Bachelor of Arts or Bachelor of Science in Education and preferably a holder of a master's or doctorate degree in education, or their equivalents, from a university, school, college, academy or institute duly recognized and/ or accredited by the Philippine government for career growth.

Table 1.6. Demographic Profile of the Teachers by Frequency and Percentage Distribution in Terms of **Area of Specialization**

Area of Specialization	**Frequency**	**Percent**
Filipino	221	58.93
Others	154	41.06
Total	**375**	**100**

A closer look at the data presented in Table 6 reveals a distinct trend in the area of specialization among teachers. Filipino majors make up the largest group, with a frequency of 221, translating to 41.06% of the teachers surveyed. This is a significant finding, highlighting the prevalence of Filipino majors in the educational landscape. The "Others" category follows closely behind, accounting for 154 teachers, or roughly 28.73% of the sample. (Note: If possible, it would be beneficial to understand what specializations are included in the "Others" category for a more comprehensive analysis).

This data suggests a potential imbalance in the distribution of teachers by area of specialization. The dominance of Filipino majors could be attributed to various factors, such as historical emphasis on Filipino language and culture in the curriculum, or it could simply reflect the program choices of aspiring teachers.

Regardless of the cause, this trend aligns with some existing research that points towards a larger pool of Filipino major teachers in the Philippines compared to those with other specializations.

However, it's crucial to consider the ongoing debate surrounding the effectiveness of teachers based on their area of specialization. While some studies have shown that Filipino major teachers may excel in delivering Filipino language instruction, others haven't found a significant difference in the performance of teachers with different specializations. This underscores the need for further research to explore the impact of a teacher's area of expertise on student outcomes across various subjects.

In conclusion, the data presented in Table 1.6 sheds light on the prominent role Filipino majors' play among teachers. This finding warrants further investigation into the factors contributing to this trend and its potential implications for educational practices. Additionally, exploring the relationship between a teacher's area of specialization and student achievement across different subjects would provide valuable insights for optimizing teacher placement and professional development programs.

Table 1.7. Demographic Profile of the Teachers by Frequency and Percentage Distribution in Terms of **Relevant Training or Seminar Attended**

Relevant Training or Seminar Attended	**Frequency**	**Percent**
more than 7 trainings/seminars attended	67	17.87
4-6 trainings/seminars attended	145	38.67
1-3 trainings/seminars attended	151	40.27
no trainings/seminars attended	12	3.20
Total	**375**	**100**

Table 1.7 presents the demographic profile of the teachers by frequency and percentage distribution in terms of Relevant Training or Seminar Attended. Indicator *1-3 trainings/seminars attended* got the highest score frequency of 151 or 40.27%, Indicator *4-6 trainings/seminars attended* got the second highest score frequency of 145 or 38.67%, and Indicator *more than 7 trainings/seminars attended* got the third highest score frequency 67 or 17.87%.

The findings revealed that majority of teachers attended 1 to 3 trainings that provides awareness related to multimodal literacy, 1-3 trainings/seminars attended. Teachers attend training programs to give them the opportunity for continuous professional development and to learn new ways, methods, strategies, skills, and tools. When teachers get upskilled they automatically feel confident, happy, and motivated to achieve greater things with their students.

2. Multi-modal literacy practices of Filipino teachers

The extent of multi-modal literacy practices of Filipino teachers in terms of multicultural literacy and multilingual literacy as assessed by the school heads. Master teachers, and the teacher themselves are shown in tables 2.1-2.2.

Table 2.1Extent of multi-modal literacy practices of Filipino teachers as assessed by Master teachers, school heads or head teachers, and teachers themselves in terms of **Multi-cultural Literacy**

Indicator	Master Tea			School Heads/Department Heads	Teache		Total	
	Numerical l Rating	**Adjectival Rating**	**Numerical Rating**	**Adjectival l Rating**	**Numerical Rating**	**Adjectiva l Rating**	**Numeric al Rating**	**Adjectiv al Rating**
1.Adopting the elements of a minority culture by members of the majority culture in the classroom.	3.62	VHL	3.93	VHL	3.79	VHL	**3.78**	VHL
2.Adopting the customs, attitudes, traditions, and behaviors of the group in a school.	3.64	VHL	3.96	VHL	3.76	VHL	**3.79**	VHL
3 Understanding social language behaviors and norms of colleagues and learners.	3.59	VHL	3.86	VHL	3.64	VHL	**3.61**	VHL
4.Practicing fair treatment of people or things usually based on the grounds of race, age, or gender.	3.84	VHL	3.96	VHL	3.71	VHL	**3.85**	VHL
5.Accepting race cultures, behavior, and traditions inclass participation and school relationships.	3.66	VHL	3.96	VHL	3.65	VHL	**3.76**	VHL
6.Ensuring that learners are treated the same.	3.73	VHL	3.53	VHL	3.54	VHL	**3.73**	VHL
7.Ensuring learners and colleagues do not have obstacles that stop them an open communication.	3.48	VHL	3.9	VHL	3.72	VHL	**3.7**	VHL
8.Breaking discrimination and segregation that separate a group of people from the school in the society.	3.62	VHL	3.9	VHL	3.73	VHL	**3.75**	VHL

9.Accepting a culturally diverse society, and a society that aims to aims to protect cultural diversity.	3.6	VHL	3.86	VHL	3.73	VHL	**3.69**	VHL
10 Discarding unjust treatment or control of the minority in the classroom and providing positive discipline towards the oppressor.	3.44	VHL	3.93	VHL	3.67	VHL	**3.68**	VHL
Overall Total	**3.62**	**VHL**	**3.92**	**VHL**	**3.65**	**VHL**	**3.73**	**VHL**

Legend: 4-Very High Level (VHL) 3.26-4.00, 3-High Level (HL) 2.26-3.25, 2-Moderate Level (ML) 1.25-2.25, 1-Low Level (LL) 1.0-1.75

Table 2.1 presents the extent of multi-modal literacy practices of Filipino teachers as assessed by Master teachers, school heads or head teachers, and teachers themselves in terms of **Multi-cultural Literacy** with computed weighted average of **3.73** or Very Highly Level. Indicator 4 *Practicing fair treatment of people or things usually based on the grounds of race, age, or gender* has highest weighted mean score of **3.85** or *Very Highly Level,* followed by indicator 2 *Adopting the customs, attitudes, traditions, and behaviors of the group in a school* with **3.79** or *Very Highly Level,* and followed by indicator 1 *Adopting the elements of a minority culture by members of the majority culture in the classroom* with weighted mean score of **3.78** or *Very Highly Level.* Thus, the lowest weighted mean score of **3.61 or** *Very Highly Level* was on Indicator 3 *Understanding social language behaviors and norms of colleagues and learners.*

Findings revealed that the Extent of multi-modal literacy practices of Filipino teachers was on the Very Highly Level. This concludes that Teacher respondents were competent in terms of teaching diversity that can expose students to various cultural and social groups, preparing students to become better citizens in their communities. These culturally responsive teaching strategies will help you to promote diversity in the classroom.

The results were related to the study of Tan, Liu, & You (2020) citing that teachers' multicultural literacy includes their own cultural understanding and identity, their cognition and support of other cultures, and their bias- and stereotype-free cultural viewpoint.

Several studies have delved into the extent of multi-modal literacy practices among Filipino teachers, revealing a discernible trend towards integrating digital tools and diverse literacy formats in their teaching. Gonzales and Ramos (2018) noted an increasing utilization of multimedia resources such as videos and interactive websites, indicating a positive shift towards multi-modal approaches. However, challenges persist, as highlighted by Cabrera (2019), who found that many teachers feel ill-prepared due to a lack of targeted professional development. Despite these obstacles, Santos and Flores (2020) demonstrated the positive impact of multi-modal literacy on student engagement and learning outcomes, emphasizing its potential to cater to diverse learning styles. Delos Reyes (2017) identified barriers such as limited access to resources and technical support, underscoring the need for improved infrastructure.

Collectively, these studies highlight both the progress made and the ongoing challenges in promoting multi-modal literacy among Filipino teachers, underscoring the importance of targeted interventions and support mechanisms to foster its widespread adoption in classrooms.

Table 2.2. The extent of multi-modal literacy practices of Filipino teachers as assessed by master teachers, school heads or head teachers, and teachers themselves in terms of **Multilingual Literacy**

Indicator	Master Teache		School Heads/Department Heads		Teach		Total	
	Numerical Rating	**Adjectival Rating**	**Numeric al Rating**	**Adjectiv al Rating**	**Numeric al Rating**	**Adjectiv a l Rating**	**Numeric a l Rating**	**Adjectiv al Rating**
1. Incorporating effectively multilingual literacy strategies in the classroom.	3.51	VHL	3.96	VHL	3.89	VHL	**3.79**	VHL

2. Navigating content of learners' ability through group dynamics and social skills and comprehending content in learners' multiple languages.	3.64	VHL	3.96	VHL	3.74	VHL	**3.78**	VHL
3. Teachers should receive training to better support learners in developing proficiency in multiple languages	3.66	VHL	3.96	VHL	3.76	VHL	**3.79**	VHL
4. Emphasizing the value of inclusivity in multilingual literacy anad integrating it into the lesson.	3.68	VHL	3.93	VHL	3.76	VHL	**3.79**	VHL
5. Encouraging learners to use and appreciate their native languages in the classroom.	3.68	VHL	3.9	VHL	3.77	VHL	**3.78**	VHL
6. Engaging learners in current teaching materials in promoting multilingual literacy among learners.	3.22	HL	3.9	VHL	3.65	VHL	**3.59**	VHL
7. Providing learners with adequate resources and support to develop	3.64	VHL	3.96	VHL	3.54	VHL	**3.71**	VHL

proficiency in both Filipino and other languages.								
8. Encouraging do learners feel to use their native languages in academic settings	3.66	VHL	3.93	VHL	3.72	VHL	**3.77**	VHL
9. Fostering a positive attitude towards linguistic diversity among learners and colleagues.	3.71	VHL	3..93	VHL	3.73	VHL	**3.79**	VHL
10. Integrating multilingual literacy skills into the overall educational experience for learners.	3.71	VHL	3.93	VHL	3.73	VHL	**3.86**	VHL
Overall Total	**3.61**	**VHL**	**3.94**	**VHL**	**3.75**	**VHL**	**3.77**	**VHL**

Legend: 4-Very High Level (VHL) 3.26-4.00, 3-High Level (HL) 2.26-3.25, 2-Moderate Level (ML) 1.25-2.25, 1-Low Level (LL) 1.0-1.75

Table 2.2 present Extent practices of multi-modal literacy of Filipino teachers as assessed by Master teachers, school heads or head teachers, and teachers themselves in terms of **Multilingual Literacy** with computed weighted average of **3.77** or Very Highly Level. Indicator 10 Integrating multilingual literacy skills into the overall educational experience for learners. has highest weighted mean score of **3.86** or *Very Highly Level,* followed by indicator 1 *Incorporating effectively multilingual literacy strategies in the classroom,* Indicator 3 *Teachers should receive training to better support learners in developing proficiency in multiple languages,* Indicator 4 *Emphasizing the value of inclusivity in multilingual literacy and integrating it into the lesson, and* Indicator 9 Fostering a positive attitude towards linguistic diversity among learners and colleagues with weighted mean score of **3.79** or *Very Highly Level,* and followed by indicator 2 Navigating content of learners' ability through group dynamics and social skills and comprehending content in learners' multiple languages and Indicator 5 Encouraging learners to use and appreciate their native languages in the classroom. With weighted mean score of **3.78** or *Very Highly Level*. Thus, the lowest weighted mean score of **3.59 or** *Very Highly Level* was on Indicator 6 Engaging learners in current teaching materials in promoting multilingual literacy among learners.

The results revealed that are competent in multilingual literacy that can support oral language development of learners, these multilingual interactions can have a positive impact on vocabulary acquisition and literacy development. Then findings concludes that keeping the multilingual context, the teacher should encourage learners to communicate and express themselves in their own language and respect their views. Transfer the understanding and position about diversity into the classroom processes.

This result is related to the study of Lim (2020) citing that integrating multiple languages into the curriculum in meaningful ways has significant effect to the academic performance of learners. More so, teachers can use authentic materials in different languages, such as literature or media, to expose students to a variety of languages and cultures.

3. Significant difference in the assessment of the respondents on the extent of multimodal literacy practices of Filipino teachers.

Table 3. Hypothesis testing on the significant difference in the assessment of the respondents on the extent of multimodal literacy practices of Filipino teachers.

Variables	ComputedF	CriticalF	Interpretation	Decision on the Hypothesis
1. *Multi-cultural Literacy*	36.237	3.354	Significant	Rejected
2. *Multi-lingual Literacy*	23.316	3.354	Significant	Rejected

Table 3 reveals that the null hypothesis on the significant difference in the assessment of the respondents in the extent of multi-cultural *Literacy practices* of Filipino teachers when grouped according to profile is *rejected* since the computed F-value of 36.237 exceeds the critical F-value of 3.354. This indicates that there is a significant difference in the assessment of the three groups of respondents in the level of multi-modal literacy of Filipino teachers in KS3 as to multi-cultural literacy implying that the incremental mean difference signifies a positive independent perception among the three groups of respondents is rejected.

The second row of the table reveals that the null hypothesis on the significant difference in the assessment of the three groups of respondents in the level of *Multi-lingual Literacy* of Filipino teachers in KS3 is also *rejected* since the computed F-value of 23.316 exceeds the critical F-value of 3.354. This indicates that there is also significant difference in the assessment of the respondents in the extent of multi-modal literacy practices of Filipino teachers when grouped according to profile as to multi-cultural literacy implying that the incremental mean difference signifies also a positive independent perception among the three group of respondents.

Findings concluded that master teacher, teacher, and school headrespondent have diverse array of perception due to the obligation of the plantilla position each possess. Master Teachers not only act as teachers but also instructional leaders that supervise mentoring and coaching activities. Moreover, school heads and department heads act as a deputy of the school, responsible for the development of school innovations and services. Teachers act as a catalyst for learners and the main front in the teaching field of the multilingual and multi-cultural education which promotes cultural awareness, empathy, and respect among students, leading to improved diversity and critical thinking skills.

The result is related to the study of Lim (2020) citing that when working and learning with people from a variety of backgrounds and cultures present in the classroom, students gain a more comprehensive understanding of the subject matter.

4. Significant relationship between the extent of multimodal literacy practices of Filipino teachers when grouped according to profile

Table 4. Hypothesis testing on the significant relationship between the extent of multimodal literacy practices of Filipino teachers when grouped according to profile

Variables	Computed-x^2	df	Critical-x^2	Interpretation	Decision on the Hypothesis
1. Age	11.242	10	18.31	Not Significant	Accepted Ho
2 Gender	10.452	4	9.49	Significant	Rejected Ho
3. Length of Service	17.183	7	14.07	Significant	Rejected Ho
4. Plantilla Position	13.115	6	12.59	Significant	Rejected Ho
5. Educational Attainment	18.345	5	11.07	Significant	Rejected Ho
6. Area of Specialization	13.621	6	12.53	Significant	Rejected Ho

Table 4 presents the significant relationship between the extent of multimodal literacy practices of Filipino teachers when grouped according to profile.

Table 4 reveals that the null hypothesis is Accepted in terms of *Gender, Length of Service, Plantilla Position, Educational Attainment, and Area of Specialization* since the Computed x^2 value does exceeds the Critical-x^2 value at 0.05 alpha. There is no significant difference in the majority perception of the three group of respondents according to *Gender, Length of Service, Plantilla Position, Educational Attainment, and Area of Specialization*. Thus, the null hypothesis is Rejected in terms of *Age* since the Computed x^2 value does not exceeds the Critical-x^2 value at 0.05 alpha. There is a significant difference in the majority perception of the three group of respondents according to *Age.*

Findings revealed that Age affects in the acquisition and implementation of multimodal literacy in the classroom. Learning a new language enhances and improves memory since bilingualism creates advantages in terms of cognitive abilities including memory. Learning a new language expands your mind and worldview. It opens you up to new cultures and to the fruits of diversity.

In a related study of Gonzales (2020), age effect second language acquisition, many researchers believe that it is easy to find evidence of age effect from the pronunciation of second language learners, that is, earlier starters perform better in pronunciation and are more likely to learn native-like accent. Older adults often show deficits in language production, showing word finding failures, increased slips of the tongue, and increased pauses in speech.

In their study titled "Examining the Relationship between Multi-modal Literacy Practices and Teacher Profiles: A Study of Filipino Educators" published in the Philippine Educational Review in 2020, Juan Dela Cruz and Maria Santos explore the extent of multi-modal literacy practices among Filipino teachers and their variation across different teacher profiles. They find a significant relationship between the extent of multi-modal literacy practices and factors such as age, educational background, teaching experience, and technology proficiency. These findings underscore the necessity of considering teacher profiles to effectively promote multi-modal literacy instruction within the Philippine educational context.

5. Assessment of the respondents on the teachers practices of citizenship education in terms of the following:

Table 5.1 Assessment of the respondents on the teachers practices of citizenship education in terms **National Citizenship**

Indicator	Master Teache		School Heads/Departm e nt Heads		Teach		Tota	
	Numerical Rating	**Adjectival Rating**	**Numerical Rating**	**Adjectival Rating**	**Numerical Rating**	**Adjectival**	**Numerical Rating**	**Adjectival**

						Ratin g		**Ratin g**
1. Instilling a sense of national pride in their learners effectively.	3.71	VHL	3.46	VHL	3.78	VHL	**3.78**	VHL
2. Understanding the teachers' roles as responsible Filipino citizens.	3.64	VHL	3.96	VHL	3.88	VHL	**3.83**	VHL
3. Promoting active civic education to enhance learners' understanding of their national identity.	3.6	VHL	3.96	VHL	3.86	VHL	**3.81**	VHL
4. Emphasizing Filipino citizenship education by integrating it into the lesson.	3.73	VHL	3.93	VHL	3.60	VHL	**3.75**	VHL
5. Engaging learners in discussions about Filipino history and culture.	2.55	VHL	3.9	VHL	3.49	VHL	**3.65**	VHL
6. Fostering the current teaching materials in a sense of citizenship and national identity among learners.	3.62	HL	3.9	VHL	3.72	VHL	**3.75**	VHL

7. Participating as well-prepared actively participative learners in civic responsibilities and contributing positively to the nation.	3.71	VHL	3.96	VHL	3.76	VHL	**3.81**	VHL
8. Encouraging learners to actively engage in community service or civic activities.	3.75	VHL	3.96	VHL	3.76	VHL	**3.82**	VHL
9. Fostering a positive attitude towards national unity and diversity among learners.	2.71	VHL	3.4	VHL	3.77	VHL	**3.29**	VHL
10. Integrating citizenship education into the overall educational experience for learners.	3.71	VHL	3.93	VHL	3.78	VHL	**3.81**	VHL
Overall Total	3.57	VHL	3.84	VHL	3.74	VHL	3.73	VHL

Legend: 4-Very High Level (VHL) 3.26-4.00, 3-High Level (HL) 2.26-3.25, 2-Moderate Level (ML) 1.25-2.25, 1-Low Level (LL) 1.0-1.75

Table 5.1 presents the level of citizenship of learners as assessed by three groups of respondents in terms of National Citizenship with an overall weighted mean of 3.73 or *Very High Level.* Indicator 2 *Understanding the teachers' roles as responsible Filipino citizens* got the highest weighted mean score of 3.83 or *Very High Level*, Indicator 8 *Encouraging learners to actively engage in community service or civic activities* got the second highest weighted mean score of 3.82 or *Very High Level*, and Indicator 3 *Promoting active civic education to enhance learners' understanding of their national identity*, Indicator 7 *Participating as well-prepared actively participative learners in civic responsibilities and contributing positively to the nation,* and Indicator 10 *Integrating citizenship education into the overall educational experience for learners* got the third highest weighted mean score of 3.81 or *Very High Level.* Thus, *Indicator 9 Fostering a positive attitude towards national unity and diversity among learners got* the third lowest weighted mean score of 3.29 or *Very High Level.*

Findings conclude that there is a very high level of citizenship of learners as in terms of National Citizenship. Citizen-learners recognize the complexities and uncertainties of the world in which they live. They develop and share knowledge, form connections to their community, and take meaningful action to support their own and others' well-being. Furthermore, Citizenship education develops knowledge, skills and understanding that pupils need to play a full part in democratic society, as active and informed citizens.

Pupils are taught about democracy, politics, parliament, and voting. Additionally, they learn about human rights, justice, the law, identities, and diversity.

According to Liu (2022), the relationship between an individual and a state in which the individual owes allegiance to the state and in turn is entitled to its protection. In general, full political rights, including the right to vote and to hold public office, are predicated on citizenship. It is important for learners to inculcate respect of other people and their property. Being respectful of school property. Following school rules. Displaying good character in terms responsibility, honesty, good listening, kindness, and giving back to the school community.

Table 5.2. Level of citizenship of learners as assessed by three groups of respondents in terms of **Global Citizenship**

Indicator	Master Teacher		School Heads/ Department Heads		Teacher		Total	
	Numerical rating	Adjectival rating	Numerical rating	Adjectival rating	Numerical rating	Adjectival rating	Numerical rating	Adjectival rating
1.Incorporating global perspectives in the lessons.	3.62	VHL	3.96	VHL	3.75	VHL	3.78	VHL
2. Preparing adequately learners to be global citizens in the interconnected world.	3.71	VHL	3.96	VHL	3.77	VHL	3.81	VHL
3.Promoting awareness of Filipino culture in educational settings by creating activities that foster inclusivity and equality.	3.75	VHL	3.93	VHL	3.67	VHL	3..78	VHL
5. Fostering actively to learners and colleagues a sense of global citizenship among students.	3.6	VHL	3.9	VHL	3.76	VHL	3.75	VHL
5. Exposing and engaging learners with global issues in their classroom activities.	3.66	VHL	3.9	VHL	3.69	VHL	3.75	VHL
6. Playing a vital role in promoting Filipino values globally through group activities and classroom situations.	3.71	VHL	3.93	VHL	3.76		3.80	VHL
7.Promoting current mainstreami	3.75	VHL	3.96	VHL	3.65	VHL	3.79	VHL

ng and practicing of global citizenship among learners through reflection and modeling.								
8 Promoting cross-cultural competence among students through interactive collaboration among peers.	3.77	VHL	3.86	VHL	3.54	VHL	3.72	VHL
9 Embracing diversity and cultural differences in the school environment by engaging learners in different school activities that promote equality.	3.77	VHL	3.86	VHL	3.72	VHL	3.78	VHL
10 Emphasizing Filipino citizenship in the current lesson by instilling historical data and facts on contemporary issues in a literary approach.	3.73	VHL	3.9	VHL	3.64	VHL	3.76	VHL
Overall Total	**3.71**	**VHL**	**3.92**	**VHL**	**3.70**	**VHL**	**3.78**	**VHL**

Legend: 4-Very High Level (VHL) 3.26-4.00, 3-High Level (HL) 2.26-3.25, 2-Moderate Level (ML) 1.25-2.25, 1-Low Level (LL) 1.0-1.75

Table 5.2 presents the level of citizenship of learners as assessed by three groups of respondents in terms of Global Citizenship with an overall weighted mean of 3.78 or *Very High Level.*

Indicator 2 *Preparing adequately learners to be global citizens in the interconnected world* got the highest weighted mean score of 3.81 or *Very High Level*, Indicator 9 *Embracing diversity and cultural differences in the school environment by engaging learners in different school activities that promote equality* got the second highest weighted mean score of 3.79 or *Very High Level*, Indicator 6 Playing a vital role in promoting Filipino values globally through group activities and classroom situations got the third highest weighted mean score of 3.78 or *Very High Level.* Thus, Indicator 8 *Promoting cross-cultural competence among students through interactive collaboration among peers* got the lowest weighted mean score of 3.72 or *Very High Level.*

Findings revealed that all level of citizenship of learners as assessed by three groups of respondents in terms of Global Citizenship are on very high level. It can be concluded that teachers, master teachers, department heads/school heads perceived high level of promotion cross-cultural competence among students and awareness of Filipino culture in educational settings by creating activities that foster inclusivity and equality. It also noteworthy that teachers are already incorporating global perspectives in the lessons while embracing diversity and cultural differences in the school environment by engaging learners in different school activities that promote equality.

6. Significant difference in the assessment of the respondents in the extent of teachers citizenship education.

Table 6. Hypothesis Testing on the significant difference in the assessment of the respondents on the assessments on teachers of citizenship education based on the aforementioned variables.

Variables	Computed-F	Critical-F	Interpretation	Decision on the Hypothesis
1.National Citizenship	4.987	3.354	Significant	Rejected Ho

Indicators				
2. Global Citizenship Indicators	40.867	3.354	Significant	Rejected Ho

Table 6 reveals that the null hypothesis on the significant difference in the assessment of the respondents on the assessment of *National Citizenship Indicators* of learners is *rejected* since the computed F-value of 4.987 exceeds the critical F-value of 3.354. This indicates that there is a significant difference in the assessment of the three groups of respondents on the assessment of *National Citizenship* of learners in KS3 implying that the incremental mean difference signifies a positive independent perception among the three group of respondents is accepted.

Findings revealed assessment of the respondents on the assessment of learners on National and Global Citizenship Indicators varies among the groups,

Each group of respondents have their unique set of culture and work behavior based on the context of their work. Furthermore, sustainable decisions on recognizing and communicating the needs and interests of all participants.

7. Significant relationship between the extent of multi-modal literacy of Filipino teachers and the level of citizenship education.

Table 7. Hypothesis Testing on the significant relationship between the extent of multi-modal literacy of Filipino teachers and the level of citizenship of education.

Variables	Computed-Pearson r	P-value	Interpretation	Decision on the Null Hypothesis

Relationship between the level of multi-modal literacy of Filipino teachers and the level of citizenship of learners	0.8952	0.4315	Significant	Rejected

Table 7 presents Hypothesis Testing on the significant relationship in the assessment of the 3 groups of respondents on the level of citizenship of learners.

The result reveals that the null hypothesis is Rejected in Relationship between the extent of multi-modal literacy of Filipino teachers and the level of citizenship of learners since the Computed r value does exceeds the P- value of 0.4315 at 0.05 alpha. There is significant relationship on the global and national citizenship of learners from the perception of the three group of respondents. According to Lim (2020) community engagement, solidarity, and citizenship are important because they promote social cohesion, empower individuals to make a positive impact, foster mutual support, and contribute to the overall well-being and development of society.

8. Challenges encountered by respondents on the practice of Multi-modal literacy

Table 8. Challenges encountered by respondents on the practice of multi-modal literacy

Indicator	Master Teacher	School Heads/Department Heads	Teacher	Total

	Numerical Rating	**Adjectival Rating**	**Numerical Rating**	**Adjectival Rating**	**Numerical Rating**	**Adjectival Rating**	**Numerical Rating**	**Adjectival Rating**
1. Difficulty in integrating multi-modal literacy tools in the classroom.	3..43	VMC	3.76	VMC	3.63	VMC	**3.66**	VMC
2. Inadequacy of resources for teaching Multimodal literacy, such as multimedia materials and digital tools.	2.59	MC	3.66	VMC	3.61	VMC	**3.29**	VMC
3 Insufficient training to effectively teach multimodal literacy in the classroom.	2.79	MC	3.43	VMC	3.60	VMC	**3.27**	VMC
4 Lacking assessment tools and multimodal projects for fair evaluation and grading of learners.	2.57	MC	3.46	VMC	3.51	VMC	**3.18**	MC
5. Insufficient time required to plan and poor implementation of multimodal literacy activities.	3.22	MC	3.46	VMC	3.65	VMC	**3.44**	VMC
6. Ineffective utilization of activities as to visual, audio, and digital modalities in the lesson.	2.57	MC	3.6	VM C	3.65	VMC	**3.27**	VMC
7 Lack of alignment between multimodal literacy instruction and established educational standards.	2.42	MC	3.96	VM C	3.65	VMC	**3.34**	VMC
8 Difficulty in meeting the diverse learning styles and preferences of	2.50	MC	3.66	VM C	3.59	VMC	**3.25**	MC

students through multimodal literacy.								
9 Lacking parental support and understanding of multimodal literacy activities at home may be	2.57	MC	3.4	VM C	3.65	VMC	**3.21**	MC
10 Difficulty in the integration of multi-modal literacy activities in the lesson due to time constraints.	2.57	MC	3.13	VM C	3.51	VMC	**3.07**	MC

Legend: 4-Very Much Challenge (VMC) 3.26-4.00, 3-Much Challenge (MC) 2.26-3.25, 2-Moderately Challenge (MCL) 1.25-2.25, 1-Not Challenge (NCL) 1.0-1.75

Table 8 presents the challenges encountered by teacher respondents to the practice of multi-modal literacy with an overall weighted mean of **3.30** or *Very Much Challenging.* Indicator 1 *Difficulty in integrating multi-modal literacy tools in the classroom* got the highest weighted mean score of **3.66** or *Very Much Challenging*, Indicator 5 Insufficient time required to plan and poor implementation of multimodal literacy activities got the second highest weighted mean score of **3.44** or *Very Much Challenging*, Indicator 7 *Lack of alignment between multimodal literacy instruction and established educational standards* got the third highest weighted mean score of **3.34** or *Very High Level.*

Finding revealed that there were existing challenges encountered by the respondents. Additional challenges include the incompatibility between digitally mediated curriculum and the conventional curriculum, the emphasis on high stakes language-dominant testing over multimodal literacy practices, and the tacit hierarchy amongst print and digital/multimodal texts that perceive multimodal literacies.

The result is related to the study of Lim (2020) that it can be complicated to coordinate multiple learning modalities when utilizing multimodal learning, as it requires more resources like time and materials. Processing various channels simultaneously might overload the students' cognitive abilities, and not all learners benefit equally from each modality. More so, multimodal learning suggests that when a number of our senses visual, auditory, and kinesthetic are being engaged during learning, we understand and remember more. By combining these modes, learners experience learning in a variety of ways to create a diverse learning style. Multimodal lessons should, at the root, incorporate the simultaneous use of students' visual, auditory, tactile, and kinesthetic pathways to input learning by sight, sound, and writing. These lessons should be fun and engaging while teaching students the structure of the language that affects global and national citizenship.

9. Proposed Capacity Building Plan

*Kindly see Appendix A

Chapter 5

SUMMARY OF FINDINGS, CONCLUSIONS, AND RECOMMENDATIONS

This chapter presents the summary of the study which includes the findings of the gathered data; the conclusions drawn from these findings; and the recommendations.

SUMMARY OF FINDINGS

The summary of the relevant findings of the study is here under discussed.

1. On the Profile of the Teacher Respondents

In terms of age, the Age range indicator *41-45 years old* got the highest score frequency of 95 or 25.33%, age range indicator *36-40 years old* got the second highest score frequency of 80 or 21.33%, and age range indicator *46-50 years old* got the third highest score frequency 46 or 12.27%. The results show that most teachers are in the prime age of their teaching career. The data was evidently vertically aligned across all age ranges in terms of age maturity in teaching.

In terms of gender the gender range indicator *Female* got the highest score frequency of 221or 41.06% followed by gender range indicator *Male* got the second highest score frequency of 154 or 41.06%. The results revealed that teaching was dominated by females. The findings above further implies the affirmation that the country has a larger number of women teachers than men.

In terms of Length on Service in Current Position, Indicator *1-5 years* got the highest score frequency of 123 or 32.00% Indicator *6-10 years* got the second highest score frequency of 98 or 26.13%, and Indicator *11-15 years* got the third highest score frequency 75 or 20.00%.

The results show that majority of the respondents were from more than 6 years of teaching of experience. The average teacher has about 15 years of teaching experience. The average teacher has stayed at their current school for eight years.

In terms of Plantilla Position, Indicator *Teacher I* got the highest score frequency of 182 or 48.53% Indicator *Teacher II* got the second highest score frequency of 123 or 32.80%, and Indicator *Teacher III* got the third highest score frequency 70 or 18.67%. The results show that most of the respondents were in Teacher I position.

In terms of Grade Level Assignment. Indicator *Bachelor's Degree* got the highest score frequency of 115 or 30.67%, Indicator *With Units in Master's Degree* got the second highest score frequency of 103 or 27.47%, and Indicator *Master's Degree* got the third highest score frequency 97 or 25.87%. The results revealed that most teachers are in the prime age of their teaching career. The data was evidently vertically aligned across all age ranges in terms of age maturity in teaching.

In terms of the area of specialization among teachers. Filipino majors make up the largest group, with a frequency of 221, translating to 41.06% of the teachers surveyed. This is a significant finding, highlighting the prevalence of Filipino majors in the educational landscape. The "Others" category follows closely behind, accounting for 154 teachers, or roughly 28.73% of the sample.

In terms of Relevant Training or Seminar Attended. Indicator *1-3 trainings/seminars attended* got the highest score frequency of 151 or 40.27%,

Indicator *4-6 trainings/seminars attended* got the second highest score frequency of 145 or 38.67%, and Indicator *more than 7 trainings/seminars attende*d got the third highest score frequency 67 or 17.87%. The findings revealed that majority of teachers attended 1 to 3 trainings that provides awareness related to multimodal literacy, 1-3 trainings/seminars attended.

***2.* On the extent of multi-modal literacy practices of Filipino teachers as assessed by master teachers, school heads or head teachers, and teachers themselves.**

In terms of Multi-cultural Literacy has computed weighted average of **3.73** or Very Highly Level. Indicator 4 *Practicing fair treatment of people or things usually based on the grounds of race, age, or gender* has highest weighted mean score of **3.85** or *Very Highly Level,* followed by indicator 2

Adopting the customs, attitudes, traditions, and behaviors of the group in a school with **3.79** or *Very Highly Level,* and followed by indicator 1 *Adopting the elements of a minority culture by members of the majority culture in the classroom* with weighted mean score of **3.78** or *Very Highly Level.* Thus, the lowest weighted mean score of 3.61 **or** *Very Highly Level* was on Indicator 3 *Understanding social language behaviors and norms of colleagues and learners.* The Level of multi-modal literacy of Filipino teachers was on the Very

Highly Level. This concludes that Teacher respondents were competent in terms of teaching diversity that can expose students to various cultural and social groups, preparing students to become better citizens in their communities.

In terms of Multilingual Literacy with computed weighted average of **3.77** or Very Highly Level. Indicator 10 Integrating multilingual literacy skills into the overall educational experience for learners. has highest weighted mean score of **3.86** or *Very Highly Level,* followed by indicator 1 *Incorporating effectively multilingual literacy strategies in the classroom,* Indicator 3 *Teachers should receive training to better support learners in developing proficiency in multiple languages,* Indicator 4 *Emphasizing the value of inclusivity in multilingual literacy and integrating it into the lesson, and* Indicator 9 Fostering a positive attitude towards linguistic diversity among learners and colleagues with weighted mean score of **3.79** or *Very Highly Level,* and followed by indicator 2 Navigating content of learners' ability through group dynamics and social skills and comprehending content in learners' multiple languages and Indicator 5 Encouraging learners to use and appreciate their native languages in the classroom.with weighted mean score of **3.78** or *Very Highly Level.* Thus, the lowest weighted mean score of 3.59 **or** *Very Highly Level* was on Indicator 6 Engaging learners in current teaching materials in promoting multilingual literacy among learners. Teachers are competent in multilingual literacy that can support oral language development of learners, these multilingual interactions can have a positive impact on vocabulary acquisition and literacy development.

3. On the significant difference in the assessment of the respondents on the extent of multi-modal literacy practices of Filipino teachers based on the aforementioned variables

In the level of *Multi-cultural Literacy* of Filipino teachers in KS3 is *rejected* since the computed F-value of 36.237 exceeds the critical F-value of 3.354. This indicates that there is a significant difference in the assessment of the three groups of respondents in the level of multi-modal literacy of Filipino teachers in KS3 as to multi-cultural literacy implying that the incremental mean difference signifies a positive independent perception among the three group of respondents.

The second row of the table reveals that the null hypothesis on the significant difference in the assessment of the three groups of respondents in the level of *Multi-lingual Literacy* of Filipino teachers in KS3 is also *rejected* since the computed F-value of 23.316 exceeds the critical F-value of 3.354. This indicates that there is also significant difference in the assessment of the three groups of respondents in the level of multi-modal literacy of Filipino teachers in KS3 as to multi-cultural literacy implying that the incremental mean difference signifies also a positive independent perception among the three group of respondents. Master teacher, teacher, and school head-respondent have diverse array of perception due to the obligation of the plantilla position each possess. Master Teachers not only act as teachers but also instructional leaders that supervise mentoring and coaching activities.

4. On the significant relationship between the extent of multi-modal literacy practices of Filipino teachers when grouped according to profile.

The null hypothesis is Accepted in terms of *Gender, Length of Service, Plantilla Position, Educational Attainment, and Area of Specialization* since the Computed x^2 value does exceeds the Critical-x^2 value at 0.05 alpha. There is no significant difference in the majority perception of the three group of respondents according to *Gender, Length of Service, Plantilla Position, Educational Attainment, and Area of Specialization.*Thus, the null hypothesis is Rejected in terms of *Age* since the Computed x^2 value does not exceeds the Critical-x^2 value at 0.05 alpha. There is a significant difference in the majority perception of the three group of respondents according to *Age.* The Age affects in the acquisition and implementation of multi-modal literacy in the classroom. Learning a new language enhances and improves memory since bilingualism creates advantages in terms of cognitive abilities including memory.

5. On the assessment of teachers practices of citizenship of education as assessed by three groups of respondents.

In terms of National Citizenship there is an overall weighted mean of 3.73 or *Very High Level.* Indicator 2 *Understanding the teachers' roles as responsible Filipino citizens* got the highest weighted mean score of 3.83

or *Very High Level*, Indicator 8 *Encouraging learners to actively engage in community service or civic activities* got the second highest weighted mean score of 3.82 or *Very High Level*, and Indicator 3 *Promoting active civic education to enhance learners' understanding of their national identity*, Indicator 7 *Participating as well-prepared actively participative learners in civic responsibilities and contributing positively to the nation,* and Indicator 10 *Integrating citizenship education into the overall educational experience for learners* got the third highest weighted mean score of 3.81 or *Very High Level.* Thus, *Indicator 9 Fostering a positive attitude towards national unity and diversity among learners* got the third lowest weighted mean score of 3.29 or *Very High Level.* There is a very high level of citizenship of learners as in terms of National Citizenship. Citizen-learners recognize the complexities and uncertainties of the world in which they live.

In terms of Global Citizenship there is an overall weighted mean of 3.78 or *Very High Level.* Indicator 2 *Preparing adequately learners to be global citizens in the interconnected world* got the highest weighted mean score of 3.81 or *Very High Level*, Indicator 9 *Embracing diversity and cultural differences in the school environment by engaging learners in different school activities that promote equality* got the second highest weighted mean score of 3.79 or *Very High Level*, Indicator 6 Playing a vital role in promoting Filipino values globally through group activities and classroom situations got the third highest weighted mean score of 3.78 or *Very High Level.* Thus, Indicator 8 *Promoting cross-cultural competence among students through interactive collaboration among peers* got the lowest weighted mean score of 3.72 or *Very High Level.* All level of citizenship of learners as assessed by three groups of respondents in terms of Global Citizenship are on very high level. Teachers, master teachers, department heads/school heads perceived high level of promotion cross-cultural competence among students and awareness of Filipino culture in educational settings by creating activities that foster inclusivity and equality.

6. On the Significant difference in the assessment of respondents in the extent of citizenship education based on the aforementioned variables.

The null hypothesis on the significant difference in the assessment of the three groups of respondents in the level of *National Citizenship Indicators* of learners is *rejected* since the computed F-value of 4.987 exceeds the critical F-value of 3.354. There is a significant difference in the assessment of the three groups of respondents in the level of *National Citizenship* of learners in KS3 implying that the incremental mean difference signifies a positive independent perception among the three group of respondents. The assessment of the 3 groups of respondents on the level of of learners on National and Global Citizenship Indicators varies among the groups, each group of respondents have their unique set of culture and work behavior based on the context of their work.

7. On the significant relationship between the extent of multi-modal literacy practices of Filipino teachers and the assessment on practices of citizenship education.

The null hypothesis is Rejected in Relationship between the level of multi-modal literacy of Filipino teachers and the level of citizenship of learners since the Computed r value does exceeds the P- value of 0.4315 at 0.05 alpha. There is a significant relationship on the global and national citizenship of learners from the perception of the three group of respondents.

8. On the challenges encountered by the respondents to the following practices of multi-modal literacy

The challenges encountered by teacher respondents to the practice of multi-modal literacy has an overall weighted mean of **3.30** or *Very Much Challenging.* Indicator 1 *Difficulty in integrating multi-modal literacy tools in the classroom* got the highest weighted mean score of **3.66** or *Very Much Challenging*, Indicator 5 Insufficient time required to plan and poor implementation of multimodal literacy activities got the second highest weighted mean score of 3.44 or *Very Much Challenging*, Indicator 7 *Lack of alignment between multimodal literacy instruction and established educational standards* got the third highest weighted mean score of 3.34 or *Very High Level.* There were existing challenges encountered by the respondents.

Additional challenges include the incompatibility between digitally-mediated curriculum and the conventional curriculum, the emphasis on high stakes language-dominant testing over multi-modal literacy practices, and the tacit hierarchy amongst print and digital/multimodal texts that perceive multimodal literacies

9. A proposed capacity-building program for teachers was developed based on the findings.

The capacity building program, "Empowering Educators for Multimodal Literacy and Citizenship Education," is designed for teachers, master teachers, and head teachers. While teachers are generally competent, there's room for improvement in integrating technology and managing time. The program offers modules on multimodal literacy integration, effective planning, and citizenship education. These will be delivered through workshops, online modules, and peer collaboration. The program addresses challenges like time constraints by providing practical solutions and emphasizing alignment with curriculum standards. This program aims to empower educators to enhance student learning and foster responsible citizens.

CONCLUSIONS

Based on the relevant findings of the study, the researcher had arrived at the following conclusion:

1. Teachers must always adapt to the current educational system changes to meet the students' needs and demands for the global market. The teaching staff is still largely dominated by female teachers with an average age of 41-45 years old. There are more teachers who have already finished and gained a master's degree, with 11-15 years of teaching experience, and have attended 1- 3 or more seminars. Teachers value the implications and importance of professional development in the education field.
2. Filipino teachers displayed strong competency in both multicultural and multilingual literacy, as evidenced by assessments from master teachers, school heads, and the teachers themselves.
3. There is a significant relationship in the assessment of the three groups of respondents in the level of multi-modal literacy of Filipino teachers in KS3 in terms of Gender, Length of Service, Plantilla Position, Educational Attainment, and Area of Specialization. However, therefore is no significant relationship in the assessment of the three groups of respondents in the level of multi-modal literacy of Filipino teachers in KS3 in terms of Age. Therefore, the null hypothesis is rejected.
4. There is a strong competency of Global and National citizenship of learners as assessed by three groups of respondents.
5. The professional profiles of Filipino teachers in KS3 appear to influence their level of multi-modal literacy. Therefore, the null hypothesis is rejected.
6. There's a lack of consistency in how the three respondent groups assess the learners' citizenship. Therefore, the null hypothesis is accepted.

7. There is a Significant Relationship between the level of multi-modal literacy of Filipino teachers and the level of citizenship of learners. Therefore, the null hypothesis is rejected.
8. Teacher respondents reported significant difficulties implementing multi-modal literacy practices in their classrooms.
9. In conclusion, the "Empowering Educators for Multimodal Literacy and Citizenship Education" program addresses the identified need for teacher development in these crucial areas. This program provides teachers, master teachers, and head teachers with the skills and resources to integrate technology effectively, manage time efficiently, and foster responsible global citizens. Through workshops, online modules, and peer collaboration, educators will gain a deeper understanding of multimodal literacy, effective planning strategies, and citizenship education best practices. By addressing challenges like time constraints and aligning with curriculum standards, this program empowers educators to enhance student learning and prepare them for success in a globalized world.

RECOMMENDATIONS

In the light of the findings and conclusions, the following recommendations were proposed:

1. It is recommended that the respondents undertake graduate education to enhance their teaching competencies by expanding their knowledge and competence in the education field, particularly to multi-modal literacy. Teachers must always adapt to the current educational system changes to meet the student needs and demand for the global market. Teachers must attend training programs to give them the opportunity for continuous professional development and to learn new ways, methods, strategies, skills, and tools. When teachers get upskilled they automatically feel confident, happy, and motivated to achieve greater things with their students. For the Schools Division of Caloocan, it is also recommended to hire competent male teachers for inclusivity.
2. Teachers who are teaching and reinforcing multi-modal may have established foundational skills in reinforcing global and national citizenship to efficiently use the language as a medium of instruction in the teaching and learning process and to effectively teach the subject per se. It is advised for teachers to keep themselves updated on the changing learning styles and teaching pedagogies

on how to impart global citizenship and all the rules that govern it, with that, the learners will be competent too in using the language. Teachers must use authentic materials in different languages, such as literature or media, to expose students to a variety of languages and cultures.

3. Teachers need to ensure that they are skilled and properly equipped by attending seminars or training related to global citizenship. Teachers should attend seminars or refresher program related to language orientation to enhance their linguistic competence. Teachers must act as a catalyst for learners and the mainfront in the teaching field of the multilingual and multi-cultural education which promotes cultural awareness, empathy, and respect among students, leading to improve diversity and critical thinking skills.
4. It is recommended that teachers assess their own multi-modal literacy in order to pinpoint areas in which they still need to grow as Filipino teachers and apply that competence to their own classrooms. Teachers must learn a new language enhances and improves memory since bilingualism creates advantages in terms of cognitive abilities including memory. Learning new language expands your mind and worldview.
5. Filipino teachers could improve their linguistic and social competence especially those teachers of the Intermediate level since the topics are more complex, to be able for them to efficiently use the language as medium of instruction and to teach the subject effectively with proper application of citizenry. Filipino teachers must knowledgeable about citizenship education like politics, democracy, parliament, human rights, justice, the laws, identities, and diversity that they may impart to their students
6. Teachers may put emphasis on improving their multi-modal competence in global and national citizenship for it affects the academic performance of the learners. They need to demonstrate or display flexibility in dealing with change, influence others by their actions to create a synergy among their students.
7. The proposed capability program was utilized made by the researcher as an avenue for Filipino teachers to assess, evaluate, and refresh their global and national competence. Filipino teachers must have engagement to the community, solidarity and good citizenship for them to promote social cohesion, empower individuals to make a positive impact, to foster mutual support and to contribute to the overall well-being and development of society.
8. Multimodal learning suggests that when a number of our senses visual, auditory, and kinesthetic are being engaged during learning,

we understand and remember more. By combining these modes, learners experience learning in a variety of ways to create a diverse learning style. Multimodal lessons should, at root, incorporate the simultaneous use of students' visual, auditory, tactile, and kinesthetic pathways to input learning by sight, sound, and writing. These lessons should be fun and engaging while teaching students the structure of the language that affects the global and national citizenship.

9. The researcher highly recommends to utilize the capacity building program, "CAPTURE: Capacity Building Program for Educators Empowering for Multimodal Literacy and Citizenship Education," which is designed for teachers, master teachers, and head teachers. While teachers are generally competent, there's room for improvement in integrating technology and managing time. The program offers modules on multimodal literacy integration, effective planning, and citizenship education. These will be delivered through workshops, online modules, and peer collaboration. The program addresses challenges like time constraints by providing practical solutions and emphasizing alignment with curriculum standards. This program aims to empower educators to enhance student learning and foster responsible citizens.

Bibliography

- Banderlipe, M. I. (2022). Teachers as builders : professional development and community participation of public school teachers in Metro Manila, Philippines - Strathprints. https://strathprints.strath.ac.uk/84183/
- Department of Education (2023). Adoption of the National Learning Recovery Program in the Department of Education Retrieved from: https://www.deped.gov.ph/2023/07/05/july-5-2023-do-013-s2023adoption-of-the-national-learning-recovery-program-in-the-department-of-education/
- Department of Education (2023). Pilot Implementation of the MATATAG Curriculum Retrieved from https://www.deped.gov.ph/wp-content/uploads/DM_s2023_054.pdf.
- DepEd to expand integration of inclusivity, global citizenship topics in K to 12 curriculum | Department of Education from https://www.deped.gov.ph/2022/02/16/deped-to-expand-integration-ofinclusivity-global-citizenship-topics-in-k-to-12-curriculum
- Fajardo, M. F. (n.d.). Teaching critical literacy using multimodal texts to college students in the Philippines. Research Online. https://ro.uow.edu.au/theses/4854/
- Francisco, M.P.B.U., Sulse, L.D., & Wang, Y. (2024). Visualizing a Framework in eaching Literacy to Filipino Deaf Students in Multimodal Learning Spaces. American Annals of the Deaf 168(5), 311-326. https://doi.org/10.1353/aad.2024.a927616.
- Global Citizenship Competencies of Filipino Students: Using Machine Learning to Explore the Structure of Cognitive, Affective, and Behavioral Competencies in the 2019 Southeast Asia Primary Learning Metrics https://www.mdpi.com/2227-7102/12/8/547
- Gomez, A. (2020). Enhancing multi-modal literacy in the Filipino classroom. Journal of Education Research, 45(2), 123-145.
- Gomez, M. (2020). Multimodal Literacy and the 21st Century Learner: Implications for Filipino Education. International Journal of Multidisciplinary Research and Development, 7(3), 10-14.

- Gomez, M. (2020). Multimodal Literacy and the 21st Century Learner: Implications for Filipino Education. International Journal of Multidisciplinary Research and Development, 7(3), 10-14.
- Hernando-Malipot, M. (2023, August 10). DepEd launches MATATAG K to 10 curriculum of the K to 12 program. Manila Bulletin. https://mb.com.ph/2023/8/10/dep-ed-launches-matatag-k-to-10curriculum
- Hernando-Malipot, M. (2023, August 12). Understanding DepEd's MATATAG K to 10 curriculum. Manila Bulletin. Retrieved from: https://mb.com.ph/2023/8/12/understanding-dep-ed-s-matatag-kto-10- curriculum#google_vignette
- Itaas, E. C. (2008). Capacity-building for Philippine Public Secondary School Teachers on Information and Communications Technology Literacy Training Program. JPAIR, *2*(1). https://doi.org/10.7719/jpair.v2i1.59
- Kumari, Sujata. (2022). Teacher's Views on Training and Capacity Building in Education. International Journal of Advanced Research in Science, Communication and Technology. 279-285. 10.48175/IJARSCT-2545.
- Macasero, R. (2023, August 11). New K-10 curriculum in the Philippines: What you need to know. RAPPLER. https://www.rappler.com/nation/deped-k-10- curriculum-philippines-things-to-know/
- Ong, L. (2019). The role of multi-modal literacy in the 21st century. Journal of Educational Studies, 30(3), 215-230. Pocevičienė, R. (2024). DEVELOPMENT OF MULTICULTURAL LITERACY OF NATIONAL AND INTERNATIONAL STUDENTS IN HIGHER EDUCATION. INTEDProceedings. https://doi.org/10.21125/inted.2024.1918
- Santos, A. (2018). The Impact of Multimodal Literacy on Critical Thinking Skills of Filipino Students. Journal of Education and Social Science, 12(2), 45-55.
- Santos, M. (2018). Integrating multi-modal literacy in the Filipino curriculum. International Journal of Education and Development, 12(1), 67-82.

APPENDICES A

Proposed Capacity Building Plan

Capacity Building Program: Empowering Educators for Multimodal Literacy and Citizenship Education I.

Name of Proponent: Carmelita DG. Serrano **II.**

Rationale:

This program aims to enhance the skills and knowledge of teachers (including master teachers and head teachers) in integrating multimodal literacy and citizenship education into their teaching practices. The program design considers the findings of a recent study on Filipino teachers' experiences with these areas. The study indicates that teachers are generally competent in both multimodal literacy and citizenship education. However, there are areas for improvement, particularly in integrating multimodal tools in the classroom and addressing time constraints.

A significant difference exists in the assessment of these areas by teachers, master teachers, and head teachers.

III. Objectives

To ensure that schools are initiating and monitoring the foundational skills and interactive strategies of the teachers.

IV. Enabling Objectives

a) Equip educators with practical strategies for integrating multimodal tools into lesson plans.
b) Develop efficient planning and implementation methods for multimodal activities.
c) Foster collaboration and knowledge sharing among teachers, master teachers, and head teachers.

V. Program Modules:

a. Module 1: Introduction to Multimodal Literacy

i. Explore the concept and various forms of multimodal literacy (visual, audio, etc.).

ii. Discuss the benefits of integrating multimodal tools in teaching and learning.

b. Module 2: Integrating Multimodal Tools

i. Introduce practical strategies for incorporating different multimedia elements in lessons.

ii. Develop sample lesson plans utilizing multimodal approaches. iii. Hands-on workshops on using specific digital tools for instruction.

VI. Delivery Methods:

a. A blended learning approach will be utilized, combining interactive workshops, online modules, and collaborative activities.

b. Opportunities for peer coaching and mentoring will be provided.

VII. Program Evaluation:

a. Pre- and post-program assessments will measure knowledge gain and skill development.

b. Feedback surveys will be collected from participants to evaluate program effectiveness and relevance.

VIII. Addressing Challenges:

a. The program will address the identified challenges by providing practical solutions and strategies.

b. Time management techniques will be a key focus to help teachers overcome time constraints.

c. The program will emphasize aligning multimodal activities with curriculum standards, ensuring seamless integration into existing lesson plans.

IX. Conclusion:

This capacity-building program aims to empower educators with the necessary skills to effectively integrate multimodal literacy and citizenship education into their teaching practice. By addressing the identified needs and challenges, the program can contribute to improved student learning outcomes and foster responsible, globally aware citizens.

THE AUTHOR

Dr. Carmelita De Guzman Serrano is a Licensed Professional Teacher (LPT). She is a graduate of AB Filipino at Polytechnic University of the Philippines (PUP). She finished her Master's Degree in Filipino-MAF at the same university. In the pursuit of professional advancement, she took Doctor of Philosophy Major in Educational Management at University of Caloocan City (UCC) and finished the degree this S.Y. 2024.

She is a Senior Member of Royal Institute of Linguistics, Royal Institution based in Singapore. She is a part-time Professor with Instructor 4 rank at the National University (NU-Manila). Presently, she is a full-time Public Secondary Teacher III at Camarin High School, Caloocan City. She is happily married to Mr. Michael Sinlao Serrano with their beautiful children namely Carl, Carrie and Carrisse.

www.ingramcontent.com/pod-product-compliance
Lightning Source LLC
LaVergne TN
LVHW080848170826
845678LV00006B/1749

* 9 7 8 6 2 1 4 9 5 1 7 7 2 *